全国高等教育学术英语规划系列教材

学术英语阅读教程
English Reading for Academic Purposes

主　编　陶晓蓉　陆　晨
副主编　程　靖　柴　艳　胡　曦
编　者　（按姓氏拼音字母排序）
　　　　柴　艳　程　靖　胡　曦
　　　　陆　晨　陶晓蓉

本教材系2020年武汉科技大学教材建设立项项目的成果。

苏州大学出版社

图书在版编目(CIP)数据

学术英语阅读教程 = English Reading for Academic Purposes / 陶晓蓉,陆晨主编. —苏州:苏州大学出版社,2022.3
全国高等教育学术英语规划系列教材
ISBN 978-7-5672-3741-4

Ⅰ.①学… Ⅱ.①陶…②陆… Ⅲ.①英语-阅读教学-高等学校-教材 Ⅳ.①H319.4

中国版本图书馆 CIP 数据核字(2021)第 203745 号

书　　名：	学术英语阅读教程 English Reading for Academic Purposes
主　　编：	陶晓蓉　陆　晨
责任编辑：	汤定军
策划编辑：	汤定军
封面设计：	吴　钰
出版发行：	苏州大学出版社(Soochow University Press)
社　　址：	苏州市十梓街1号　邮编：215006
印　　装：	广东虎彩云印刷有限公司
网　　址：	www.sudapress.com
邮　　箱：	sdcbs@suda.edu.cn
邮购热线：	0512-67480030
销售热线：	0512-67481020
开　　本：	787 mm×1092 mm　1/16　印张：17.5　字数：399千
版　　次：	2022年3月第1版
印　　次：	2022年3月第1次印刷
书　　号：	ISBN 978-7-5672-3741-4
定　　价：	59.00元

凡购本社图书发现印装错误,请与本社联系调换。服务热线:0512-67481020

Overview

Academic English, which conveys ideas in a precise and objective manner, is a genre of English used in the world of research, study, teaching and universities. *English Reading for Academic Purposes* is intended to help learners of English, undergraduates and postgraduates in particular, to read English materials more effectively and critically by presenting and developing various skills needed for successful reading comprehension in educational settings. This book offers a wide range of authentic and academic English reading materials and is designed to assist students to comprehend, examine, question, and evaluate the issues arising in academic English contexts.

Structure and Focus of the Book

This book is organized into 10 units, with the first 5 units focusing on the themes of general interest and the last 5 units targeting on the topics of specialized areas. Each unit contains:

- A specific topic
- Learning outcomes
- Two reading passages
- Reading comprehension strategies
- Language spotlight
- Vocabulary practice
- Critical thinking tasks
- Glossary of the unit

Each unit concludes with an extended reading passage related to the unit theme, which is aimed at providing a wider range of academic texts for students to reinforce their academic reading skills acquired from the study of the unit.

Activities for Each Unit

The articles selected in *English Reading for Academic Purposes* involve a number of essential academic features that are well presented throughout the activities designed for the book. Each of the two reading passages in each unit includes the following tasks:

Task A Reading Comprehension Strategies

Reading is a thinking process. Effective readers use strategies to understand what they read before, during, and after reading. This activity offers typical reading strategies for students to become independent readers in academic English contexts. These strategies include: previewing, predicting, skimming, scanning, making inferences, recognizing organizational patterns, using context to find meaning, reading critically, etc.

Task B Language Spotlight

Grammar and sentence patterns are taught within readings to enhance students' reading comprehension ability, particularly in academic English contexts, by dealing with such language skills as comparative and contrasting structures, language for describing trends and statistics, cause and effect language, styles of citation, passive voice, language for definitions and explanations, cohesive language, hedging language, and impersonal style for stating aims.

Task C Vocabulary Practice

Academic vocabulary refers to words that are typically used in academic English settings. This activity focuses on key aspects of academic vocabulary identified from each passage, and provides expanded vocabulary practice including collocations, adjectives for classifying and evaluating concepts, adverbials to signal a stance, reporting verbs for citation, prefixes and suffixes for building complex words, etc.

Task D Critical Thinking

Critical thinking is the ability to think clearly and rationally, and it is about understanding the logical connection between ideas. This task draws students attention to the areas like reflecting on the topic of a passage, evaluating the content of a passage, identifying perspective and stance of an author, recognizing organizational patterns, differing facts from opinions, etc.

Glossary of the Unit

This section focuses on the target vocabulary items from the two reading passages in each unit, including their pronunciation, definition, example sentences, collocations and phrases, which will help learners to review the unit's target vocabulary.

Pacing Guide

One unit of *English Reading for Academic Purposes* takes about 8 – 10 class hours to complete. All 10 units require approximately 80 – 100 class hours, assuming that the teacher covers the two reading passages in each unit with a range of tasks and activities, but sets aside all the extended reading passages as homework.

Contents

1A

Unit 1 Fresh Start on Campus
Reading 1: Going to University? Advice for Freshers / 3
Reading 2: What Is Freshers' Week? / 12
Extended Reading: Why Are "Tents of Love" Popping Up in Chinese Colleges?
  / 22

Unit 2 Thinking on Education
Reading 1: US Higher Education Challenges / 29
Reading 2: The Child-Driven Education—"Hole in the Wall" Experiments / 46
Extended Reading: US Colleges Fret Over Fall in Chinese Students / 60

Unit 3 Love and Friendship
Reading 1: We All Need Friends / 68
Reading 2: Differences Between Love and Friendship / 76
Extended Reading: What's the Difference Between Friendship and Love? / 84

Unit 4 Choice on Lifestyles
Reading 1: Life Has Become Harder for Young Families / 89
Reading 2: Obesity and Poor Fitness / 97
Extended Reading: Life in Ancient Cities / 108

Unit 5 Uncovered History
Reading 1: The Origins of Theater / 113
Reading 2: Lessons from the *Titanic* / 120
Extended Reading: Five Guesses on Emperor Qin Shihuang's Tomb / 131

Unit 6 Food Matters
Reading 1: A Health Report / 140

Reading 2: How Might Exercise Affect Our Food Choices and Our Weight?
/ 153

Extended Reading: UK Government Criticised Over Food Security and Poverty
/ 169

Unit 7 Business and Job Hunting
Reading 1: A Woman's Work / 173

Reading 2: Companies Are Relying More and More on Psychometric Tests / 184

Extended Reading: Some Unfortunate Mismatches in Young People's Job Preferences and Prospects / 196

Unit 8 Environmental Protection
Reading 1: A World of Plastic Pollution / 200

Reading 2: Dangers from E-waste / 209

Extended Reading: Plastic Pollution Crisis Around the World / 219

Unit 9 Science Changes Life
Reading 1: Artificial Intelligence and the Future of Humans / 224

Reading 2: Surprising Ways How Driverless Cars Will Change Our Future / 232

Extended Reading: What Is AI Technology and How Is It Used? / 240

Unit 10 Illness and Disease
Reading 1: Cold Comfort / 246

Reading 2: The Growing Global Threat of Antibiotics Resistance / 256

Extended Reading: Food and Disease / 266

Contents Map for 1A

Unit Number and Theme	Reading	Tasks			
		Reading Comprehension Strategies	Language Spotlight	Vocabulary Practice	Critical Thinking
Unit 1 Fresh Start on Campus	Reading 1: Going to University? Advice for Freshers	Previewing	Necessary elements in previewing	Adjectives related to emotions	Evaluating the effectiveness of the text
	Reading 2: What Is Freshers' Week?	Predicting	Inferring the meaning of words	Nouns related to campus life	Comparing similarities and differences
Unit 2 Thinking on Education	Reading 1: US Higher Education Challenges	Skimming for general ideas	Referencing and bibliography	Understanding key words	Debate on selected topics
	Reading 2: The Child-Driven Education—"Hole in the Wall" Experiments	Identifying the author's attitude	Verb forms for hypothesizing and speculating	Expressions for suggesting, accepting and rejecting ideas	Reflecting on the viewpoints of the text
Unit 3 Love and Friendship	Reading 1: We All Need Friends	Skimming for gist	Citations and quotations	Words with hyphens	Commenting on the friendship and love on campus
	Reading 2: Differences Between Love and Friendship	Summarizing	Language for contrasts	Verbs related to giving definitions	Contrasting between two forms of love

Unit Number and Theme	Reading	Tasks			
		Reading Comprehension Strategies	Language Spotlight	Vocabulary Practice	Critical Thinking
Unit 4 Choice on Lifestyles	Reading 1 : Life Has Become Harder for Young Families	Skimming for gist	Describing trends and statistics	Cohesive devices	Evaluating the content of a text
	Reading 2 : Obesity and Poor Fitness	Pattern of the essay	Review of referencing within an article	Reporting verbs	Reflecting on reading patterns
Unit 5 Uncovered History	Reading 1 : The Origins of Theater	Identifying essay patterns	Transitional expressions for causal analysis	Words related to theater	Summary and review
	Reading 2 : Lessons from the *Titanic*	Scanning	Summary completion	Words related to describing a cruise	Summary and comparison

Contents Map for 1B

Unit Number and Theme	Reading	Tasks			
		Reading Comprehension Strategies	Language Spotlight	Vocabulary Practice	Critical Thinking
Unit 6 Food Matters	Reading 1: A Health Report	Skimming for main ideas	Prefixes mal-, over- & suffixes -ness, -hood, -sick, -ful, -aholic	Describing food	Debate on "eating healthy food is good for our health"
	Reading 2: How Might Exercise Affect Our Food Choices and Our Weight?	Features of research reports	Academic writing style	Identifying language features of reports	Ways to lose weight
Unit 7 Business and Job Hunting	Reading 1: A Woman's Work	Features of an editorial	Metaphors	Verbs used to introduce one's opinion	Similarities and differences between cultures
	Reading 2: Companies Are Relying More and More on Psychometric Tests	Features of the illustration essay	Noun suffixes -ion & -ence	Words to describe personalities	The effectiveness of a psychological test / psychometric test
Unit 8 Environmental Protection	Reading 1: A World of Plastic Pollution	Identifying pros and cons	Identifying homonyms	Affixes	Evaluating the content of a text
	Reading 2: Dangers from E-waste	Organizing information—creating a concept map	Clarifying cause and effect	Understanding words with multiple meanings	Further evaluating the content of the text

Unit Number and Theme	Reading	Tasks			
		Reading Comprehension Strategies	Language Spotlight	Vocabulary Practice	Critical Thinking
Unit 9 Science Changes Life	Reading 1: Artificial Intelligence and the Future of Humans	Identifying logical flowing of ideas	Present participle as adverbial of result	Enlarging vocabulary by synonyms	Relationship between AI and human life
	Reading 2: Surprising Ways How Driverless Cars Will Change Our Future	Recognizing essay structure	Differences between expressions of tendency	Deducing the meaning of unfamiliar phrases	Driverless cars in real life
Unit 10 Illness and Disease	Reading 1: Cold Comfort	Chunk reading	Identifying cause and effect expressions	Learning medical words by a word splash	Distinguishing facts from opinions
	Reading 2: The Growing Global Threat of Antibiotics Resistance	Skipping over unknown words	Choosing the right level of formality	Words used to describe negative effects	Inferences and evidence

Fresh Start on Campus

Going to university is a brand-new experience. When we first come into university, we may feel excited and curious about everything, which is a fresh start. In this unit, you will get to know what freshers will experience in the UK universities. You will get some advice about study in your first year of university but also understand the meaning of freshers' week. You will learn how to preview and predict during reading, and how to infer the meaning of the words if necessary and get the skill of memorizing words.

By the end of this unit, you will be able to:

SKILL	TASK
learn the importance of previewing	• Reading 1 • Task A
learn the steps and elements of previewing	• Reading 1 • Task B
get the topic and the main idea of a text before reading	• Reading 1 • Task B
use previewing skills for the first-time reading	• Reading 1 • Task B
learn how to memorize words in a context	• Reading 1 • Task C
identify adjectives related to emotions	• Reading 1 • Task C
evaluate the effectiveness of a text	• Reading 1 • Task D
learn the process of predicting	• Reading 2 • Task A
predict important information before reading	• Reading 2 • Task A
learn approaches to inferring the meaning of new words in a context	• Reading 2 • Task B
guess the meaning of unfamiliar words in the text	• Reading 2 • Task B
identify nouns related to campus life	• Reading 2 • Task C
compare similarities and differences between two cultures	• Reading 2 • Task D

Reading 1

Going to University? Advice for Freshers

¹ Freshers' week is the week where you really get the impression of what your university life is going to be like. Once your timetable is shown, the thought of university work, lectures and study can become a bit <u>daunting</u> all at once! Having been through university and being a newly graduate, I would like to share with you some of my favourite top tips I have learnt on my university journey that I hope will help you freshers too!

² My first main piece of advice is to look after yourself physically. To have a great mindset, it's important to look after yourself on the outside as well as the inside. University is a massive step and new chapter in your life and you want to enter it with the ability to have some common sense and get to understand your routines. Eating, sleeping and exercising are all important and vital things your body needs on those long nights and days, especially if your university schedule looks pretty busy. Don't burn yourself out in the first term. Fresher's flu is a common symptom among students in the first week, typically due to the late nights, parties and staying up late to meet new people and get to know your surroundings. It can be physically and mentally <u>exhausting</u> and I know it's <u>exciting</u> but try and balance it during the week. Try and get that 20-minute power nap in if you know you're going to be out all night partying with your new friends and eat regularly to keep your energy levels up.

³ For some students, moving away from home can be quite daunting and seeing lots of new faces and new places at once can make you feel a little bit <u>homesick</u> at first. To help overcome this, I found taking loads of photos from home and placing them around my room reminded me that my friends or family weren't far away and a phone call or a visit every now and again would make me feel better. Being able to contact friends or family back home regularly

makes you realise that they haven't gone forever but you are about to embark on a new chapter in your life and make some more life-long friends along the way. Before you know it, the homesickness has gone and you are excited for new beginnings and ways of life!

[4] Remember to join social events and clubs at university, as this helps you to meet new people and get stuck into university life. It does not have to be an anxious situation but a more uplifting and exciting experience instead! Another way of getting to know your housemates is encouraging flat meals together or little outings which gives everyone the chance to get to know each other. If you live in halls, keep your bedroom door open when you want that time to socialise, you'll soon realise how many people just come in and sit on your bed for a chat with a cuppa at random hours of the day! It also helps to give you regular breaks if you're studying hard. When your door is open, it's more welcoming for others to attempt to reach out to you and you will become a more open person.

[5] Focusing on university studies can be really stressful when you have a lot of deadlines to reach. I found during times when I had a lot of work to sit down and do, I would make a checklist of everything I needed to do that week. It kept my mind clear and free of stressful and worrying situations where I would leave everything till the last minute. There are a lot of students at university that do leave everything till the last minute, but this is not a good idea. Making sure you have everything completed nice and early gives you the chance to proofread back over your work in case you've made any serious mistakes or small grammatical errors. Once I had achieved my checklist I would reward myself with social time with my friends such as a night out or a trip somewhere. Even though it may seem hard to do it at university, it's important to keep a balance of study, work, socialising, exercising, eating and sleeping. Remember, if you do feel under too much pressure at any time, there are always people who work for your university such as a welfare officer or even a close friend to talk to. Don't sit and dwell on your own, there are many of students that undergo stressful situations every day! First year does not count but it's a good way of practicing good habits and maintaining a routine that is best for you.

⁶ Remember—going to university is a massive step for anyone but it is an exciting 3 or even 4 years that you will love to look back on. Most people only go through the journey once so it's best to make it a good one and to the best you possibly can in all aspects. I found going to university built my confidence in many ways, and even though I dreaded them at first, those presentations to a big group of people seem like a breeze at the end.

⁷ On that note, I wish all of you freshers every success and make sure you feel proud of all your achievements on graduation day!

Source: Going to university? Advice for freshers. (n. d.). *Student Recipes*. Retrieved May 17, 2021, from https://studentrecipes.com/blog/going-to-university-advice-for-freshers.

Task A | Reading Comprehension Strategy: Previewing

What is previewing?

◇ ***Previewing*** is a useful and important reading strategy in class learning. ***Previewing*** can be the first-time reading by yourself, in which you may recognize how information is organized, identify main ideas, and raise questions in the text. As a result, you will understand the material better when the teacher guides you to the second-time reading in detail during class.

Discussion

Have you ever done previewing before? If yes, what kind of things have you done for previewing? Discuss with your partner.

Make some notes here to guide your discussion.	

Task B | Language Spotlight: Necessary elements in previewing

What is previewing?

➢ It is not essential for us to preview all the texts that we are interested in. Usually, *previewing is used for intensive reading*.

➢ So, first of all, we should take several steps to make a judgement whether the text is worth reading intensively. And here are the steps we should follow:

Step 1 Read the title and subtitles if there are any.
Step 2 Read the first paragraph.
Step 3 Read the last paragraph.
Step 4 Read the first sentence of each remaining paragraph.

Usually, after finishing these 4 steps, you may get the topic and the main idea of the article, then you can decide whether to further read the article according to your interest.

Elements for taking notes during previewing

➢ If you decide to do an intensive reading, then it's time for you to do your first-time reading and take notes for the following four elements:

Element 1 Notice the genre and structure of the article.
Element 2 Underline the unfamiliar vocabulary without looking up the words.
Element 3 Write down your inspiring thoughts.
Inspiring thoughts could include:
① language pattern that you think is important to learn;
② things that make you think "Wow" or "Awesome";
③ connection you can make to your life, the world or another text;
④ your favourite part.
Element 4 Raise questions if there are any.
Questions could include:
① questions related to language points (grammar, vocabulary, etc.);
② critical thinking questions related to social phenomenon.

Exercises

1. Have a quick look at the passage "Going to University? Advice for Freshers", finish Steps 1 – 4 in *Previewing*, and answer the following questions:
   1) What is the topic?
   2) What is the main idea?

Topic	Main idea

2. Now begin your first-time reading and take notes on Elements 1 – 4.

   Element 1: Genre & Structure

Genre	Structure

   Element 2: Unfamiliar Vocabulary

Unknown words/phrases

   Element 3: Inspiring Thoughts

Language pattern that you think is important to learn

Things that make you think "Wow" or "Awesome"
Connection you can make to your life, the world or another text
Your favourite part

Element 4: Questions

Questions related to language points	Critical thinking questions related to social phenomenon

Discussion

Show your notes to your partner, and exchange your understanding on the passage "Going to University? Advice for Freshers".

_____
_____
_____

Task C | Vocabulary Practice: Adjectives related to emotions

1. Think about the following questions and share your idea with your partner. You can take notes in the table.
   1) Do you like to memorize words?
   2) Do you have any good ways to memorize words?

Notes

   Usually, if we memorize words in a context, it will be much easier.

2. In this text, there are some emotional words which you can use to describe feelings. Please find the appropriate words in "Going to University? Advice for Freshers" to match with the pictures.

_____ _____ _____

_____ _____ _____

3. Here are some more adjectives related to emotions. Please classify the words according to different feelings.

| gloomy | light-hearted | cheerful | sorrowful | irritated |
| elated | joyful | delightful | depressed | annoyed |

gloomy light-hearted cheerful sorrowful irritated elated joyful delightful depressed annoyed	

4. Match the following words with definitions.

| tutor | tutorial | timetable | lecturer |
| academic | advisor | module | assessment |

1) a unit that can form part of a course of study
2) a list showing the times at which particular events will happen
3) a consideration of someone or something and a judgment about them
4) a teacher whose job is to pay special attention to the studies or health, etc. of a student or a group of students
5) a person who gives each student academic advice and guidance
6) a person who teaches at a university or college
7) a period of teaching in a university that involves discussion between an individual student or a small group of students and a tutor

Is it different from Chinese university study?

Task D | Critical Thinking: Evaluating the effectiveness of the text

Discussion

Think about the following questions and discuss with your partner. You can take notes in the table.
1. How do you think of the advice from the writer? Do you think they are effective?
2. Do you have any more problems on university study? If yes, what are they?
3. According to your experience, is there any difference between university study and high school study?

Notes

Reading 2

What Is Freshers' Week?

1 In British universities, new students have a special name: they are called Freshers, a shortened version of the American word "Freshmen". After their A-level exams, young people often make a fresh start by going to university, which can involve moving to a new city and leaving their family home. The first week of university life in the UK is called Freshers' week and is both a scary and exciting experience.

2 Freshers' week is a chance to make lots of new friends and try out different hobbies. Most universities in the UK have a Union building: a place where students go to have fun. It is the perfect place to meet friends and join university societies. I go to Leeds University, which has one of the best Unions in the country. It has a supermarket, a gift shop, two bars and even three underground nightclubs. It also hosts over 300 societies, including sports teams, political groups and a university newspaper. Students buy a membership to be part of a society and go to social events to meet others with similar interests. Sometimes there are quite a lot of students in lectures so it is difficult to get to know people in class. Therefore, each subject has its own club, for example the English Society and the Philosophy society.

3 In Freshers' week, lots of special activities are organised for people to meet each other. Tours of the town, creative workshops and parties are great ways to socialise with other Freshers. Sometimes famous singers come and play concerts especially for the new students of the university. There is also the opportunity to go on trips to theme parks or other big cities nearby.

4 Students often move into "halls of residence" in their first year. They are placed in apartments with a few other new students and usually have their own bedrooms but share a kitchen. This is an excellent way to make friends but

sometimes it can be difficult if you don't get along with your new flatmates or if the shared area gets very messy.

⁵ Freshers' week can be quite an exhausting experience because so many activities happen at once. A lot of students feel homesick when they first arrive on campus and keep themselves very busy to avoid feeling sad about leaving their family. Some students use their new liberty to drink a lot of alcohol and eat unhealthy food during Freshers' week. This can cause "Freshers' flu": people get ill after a week of late nights and non-stop parties. It is very easy to feel peer pressure during this time because people say it is supposed to be the best week of your life. It is an opportunity to make friends but it is important to remember that it is only the beginning of your time at university and that you have three years ahead of you to have fun.

Source: Eleanor, C. (2013, October 4). What is freshers' week? *British Council*. Retrieved May 17, 2021, from http://learnenglishteens.britishcouncil.org.cn/magazine/life-around-world/what-freshers-week.

Task A | Reading Comprehension Strategy: Predicting

1. Have you ever had the same experience? If yes, then tick the statement.
   1) I prefer starting reading at the beginning and going word by word.
   2) When I find unfamiliar words while reading, I would like to stop immediately to look up every unknown word until the end of reading.
   3) I try to guess the meaning of the word while reading.
   4) I can finish reading a text although I don't get the exact meaning of all the words.
   5) I can understand the text with some unfamiliar words.

> Reading is a guessing game, and here is the process of reading:
> ➢ Reading → Predicting → Reading → Proving/Disproving
> ➢ Predicting means thinking in advance about what to be read.

2. Choose all the statements about predicting which you think are right.
   1) Predicting enables us to be aware of our goal in reading.
   2) Predicting activates schema: that is, it calls into mind any experience and associated knowledge that we already have about the topic and the text.
   3) Predicting helps us to focus in the reading process.
   4) Predicting improves comprehension.

> **How to predict before reading**
> ① Looking at the title, predict about the subject of the text.
> ② According to the title and pictures on the page, predict about the content of the text: what kind of information will be introduced in the text?
> ③ Predict about writing style and content.

Exercise

1. Look at the following title, what might be the subject of the text?

2. According to the title, what kind of information do you think the text will include?

3. What is the purpose of writing this text? How do you think of the writing style? Will it be formal or informal?

Ways to Have a Healthy Lifestyle

Discussion

What kind of information can you predict before reading "What Is Freshers' Week?" Discuss with your partner and try to get as much information as possible. You can take notes in the table.

Notes

Task B | Language Spotlight: Inferring the meaning of words

> **Inferring the meaning of a word** refers to guessing the meaning of a new word, a difficult word, or a keyword based on a comprehensive understanding of the **information**, **logic**, **background knowledge**, and **language structure** of the text in the reading process.

> In this way, the reader can quickly infer the meaning of the word through the clues provided by the context or the structural characteristics of the new word itself during the reading process.

How to infer the meaning of a word

① The meaning of a new word could be inferred by using **commas**, **dashes** or **brackets** to indicate the meaning of the new word.

   e. g. Origami—Japanese paper folding—is family fun.

② The meaning of a new word could be inferred by using **attributive clauses** to indicate the meaning of the new word.

   e. g. He takes a special interest in botany which concerns the study of plants.

③ The meaning of a new word could be inferred by using expressions related to **definition** like *or, that is to say, in other words, to be, mean, refer to, be defined as, be known as, be called, be termed* to indicate the meaning of the new word.

   e. g. Nuclear war is likely to end in mutual destruction, that is, destruction in which both countries involved are destroyed.

④ The meaning of a new word could be inferred by using examples to **explain** the meaning of the new word.

   e. g. Select some periodicals like the *Detective*, *Reader's Digest*, *New York Times* and so on.

⑤ The meaning of a new word could be inferred by **contrasting expressions** in the sentence.

   e. g. Unlike her gregarious sister, Jane is a shy, unsociable person who does not like to go to parties or to make new friends.

⑥ The meaning of a new word could be inferred by using the **logical relationship** of the preceding sentence.

   e. g. The river is so turbid that it is impossible to see the bottom even when it is shallow.

⑦ The meaning of a new word could be inferred based on **common sense** or **experience**.
  e. g. He went into a hardware to buy some nails.
⑧ The meaning of a new word could be inferred according to **word formation**.
  e. g. The disappearance of the jewel aroused great concern.

Exercise

Please infer the meaning of the words by using the above ways.

1. A tariff is a duty or fee levied on goods being imported into the country.
2. My uncle used to be a prestidigitator who entertained the children by pulling rabbits out of his hat, swallowing fire, and other similar tricks.
3. It will be very hard but also very brittle—that is, it will break easily.
4. A silence in a conversation may also show stubbornness, uneasiness, or worry.
5. Mary didn't notice me when I came into the classroom, because she was completely engrossed in her reading.
6. She is usually prompt for all her class, but today she arrived in the middle of her first class.
7. Green loves to talk, and his brothers are similarly loquacious.
8. — It's really cold out tonight.
   — Sure it is. My hands are practically numb. How about lighting the furnace?
9. Bullfight is very popular in Spain.

Discussion

Circle the words that you are not familiar with in "What Is Freshers' Week", and try to infer the meaning with your partner.

Unfamiliar words	Inferring the meaning

English Reading for Academic Purposes 1A

Task C | Vocabulary Practice: Nouns related to campus life

Exercises

1. Find nouns related to campus life in "What Is Freshers' Week?" and list them here.

Nouns related to campus life

2. Create a scene with your partner and make a dialogue by using the above expressions related to campus life. You can take notes in the table.

Notes

3. Please complete the sentences using the correct words below with the appropriate form.

involve   version   host   socialise   nearby   messy   liberty

   1) I enjoy _____ with the other students.
   2) People fear that security cameras could infringe personal _____.
   3) Any investment _____ an element of risk.
   4) The car is parked _____.
   5) The English _____ of the novel is due for publication next year.
   6) The house was always _____.
   7) Germany _____ the World Cup finals.

Task D | Critical Thinking: Comparing similarities and differences

Think about the following questions and discuss with your partner. You can take notes in the table.
1. What is the first week of university like in China?
2. Are there any similarities or differences compared with the British Freshers' week?

Notes

Glossary of Unit 1

Reading 1

lecture
n. a talk that is given to a group of people to teach them about a particular subject, often as part of a university or college course
e. g. She's planning to give a series of <u>lectures</u> on modern art.

newly
adv. lately, recently
e. g. They are a <u>newly</u> married couple.

physically
adv. in a way that is connected with a person's body rather than their mind
e. g. I felt <u>physically</u> sick before the exam.

mindset
n. If you refer to someone's mindset, you mean their general attitudes and the way they typically think about things.
e. g. I try to have a positive <u>mindset</u>, keep my mind focused on what I have to do.

massive
adj. extremely large or serious
e. g. He suffered a <u>massive</u> heart attack.

routine
n. the normal order and way in which you regularly do things
e. g. Grandma gets upset if we change her <u>routine</u>.

vital
adj. necessary or essential in order for sth. to succeed or exist
e. g. The sciences are a <u>vital</u> part of the school curriculum.

symptom
n. a change in your body or mind that shows that you are not healthy
e. g. Look out for <u>symptoms</u> of depression.

typically
adv. used to say that sth. usually happens in the way that you are stating
e. g. The factory <u>typically</u> produces 500 chairs a week.

surroundings
n. everything that is around or near sb./sth.
e. g. The buildings have been designed to blend in with their <u>surroundings</u>.

mentally
adv. connected with or happening in the mind
e. g. <u>Mentally</u>, I began making a list of things I had to do.

nap
n. a short sleep, especially during the day
e. g. Tip: Take a <u>nap</u> after a heavy study session to allow your brain time to rest.

outing
n. a short trip, usually with a group of people, away from your home, school, or place of work
e. g. One evening, she made a rare <u>outing</u> to the local night club.

cuppa

n. (*BrE*) (*informal*) a cup of tea

e. g. Do you fancy a cuppa?

attempt

v. to make an effort or try to do sth., especially sth. difficult

e. g. I will attempt to answer all your questions.

checklist

n. a list of the things that you must remember to do, to take with you or to find out

e. g. Create a checklist for your kids.

proofread

v. to read and correct a piece of written or printed work

e. g. Has this document been proofread?

welfare

n. the general health, happiness and safety of a person, an animal or a group

e. g. We are concerned about the child's welfare.

dread

v. to be very afraid of sth.; to fear that sth. bad is going to happen

e. g. I dread to think what would happen if there really was a fire here.

embark on

to start to do sth. new or difficult

e. g. We'll also include some lessons learned from our experience that will hopefully help you if you decide to embark on a similar project.

dwell on

to think, speak, or write at length

e. g. This is not too serious, so I won't dwell on it.

Reading 2

fresher

n. (*BrE*) (*informal*) a student who has just started his or her first term at a university

e. g. Joe went enthusiastically to every lecture like a fresher.

involve

v. If a situation, an event or an activity involves sth., that thing is an important or necessary part or result of it.

e. g. The test will involve answering questions about a photograph.

society

n. a group of people who join together for a particular purpose

e. g. Amy is a member of the drama society.

version

n. a form of sth. that is slightly different from an earlier form or from other forms of the same thing

e. g. There are two versions of the game, a long one and a short one.

host

v. to organize an event to which others are invited and make all the arrangements for them

e. g. Mr. Marce will host a reception tonight.

socialise

v. to meet and spend time with people in a friendly way, in order to enjoy yourself

e. g. Life moves so quickly these days and though we may network or socialise with many people, we don't necessarily get to know them on a deeper level.

nearby

adv. a short distance from sb./sth.; not far

away

e. g. They live nearby.

residence

n. the place where you live

e. g. 10 Downing Street is the British Prime Minister's official residence.

apartment

n. a set of rooms for living in, usually on one floor of a building

e. g. We leased an apartment from the school.

flatmate

n. (*BrE*) a person who shares a flat/apartment with one or more others

e. g. I quarreled with my flatmate last night.

messy

adj. dirty and/or untidy

e. g. Painting a room can be messy work.

liberty

n. freedom to live as you choose without too many restrictions from government or authority

e. g. We must not restrain children of their liberty.

Extended Reading

Why Are "Tents of Love" Popping Up in Chinese Colleges?

Chinese colleges have come up with an unusual way to help freshmen settle in. They turn their gyms into campsites for moms and dads, some of whom have traveled thousands of miles across the country, to say goodbye.

For the past five years, Tianjin University in northern China has provided free accommodation for parents in what it calls "tents of love". Other schools let parents sleep on mats in school gymnasiums.

"Going to college is a life moment and my parents didn't want to miss that," said Xiong Jinqi, a freshman at Tianjin University majoring in applied chemistry. His parents traveled with him on the 19-hour train journey from Jiangxi Province in southern China. "My parents are eager to see what my life will be in the next four years."

Coddled?

Images of school gyms packed with parents have been widely shared on Chinese social media prompting a debate on whether China's only children are too coddled. Some have voiced criticism of Tianjin University, saying that they think both the parents and the children should be more independent. Of course, "helicopter parents" like these aren't confined to China.

But China's millennials are often doted on by parents and two sets of grandparents, prompting fears that China has produced a generation of "little emperors" unable or unwilling to take care of themselves.

Xiong Bingqi, the deputy director of think-tank 21st Century Education Research Institute and no relation to the Xiongs, thinks the problem is overstated. "It has always been a problem in China that at the start of every school year, colleges are packed with parents who come along to drop off their children and stay with them," he said. "For some families, it's their way to celebrate the first-ever family member who's able to go to college," Xiong added. "There's nothing wrong with sharing the happiness."

"No brainer"

Xiong's father said the decision to escort their son was a no-brainer. He and his wife are among the many "campers" who sleep in the 550 temporary tents set up in the Tianjin University gym. "My child has lots of luggage and we also want to go travel," said his father Xiong Yonghui. "The hotels nearby are fully booked so I had to sleep in the tents."

Their son also shrugged off the criticism although he said he was looking forward to living on his own for the first time. "Being accompanied by my parents doesn't mean I'm spoiled."

Source: Why "tents of love" are popping up in Chinese colleges. (2016, September 12). (n.d.). *Cable News Network*. Retrieved August 12, 2021, from https://edition.cnn.com/2016/09/12/asia/china-college-parents-tents-of-love/index.html.

Thinking on Education

In this unit you are going to think on education. You will have a further look at the topic of education, especially about issues of higher education. You will further extend your tutorial participation skills, and will practice reading skills. Also you will practice note-taking skills that are now so often used in lectures. There will be opportunities for practice of speculating and hypothesizing. And there is also a focus on the expressions for suggesting, accepting and rejecting ideas that you may have to use in the tutorial discussions with your classmates, lecturers and other staff during your further studies.

By the end of this unit, you will be able to:

SKILL	TASK
increase general knowledge about the current issues of higher education and critically consider it globally	• Speaking • Tasks A, B • Reading 1 • Tasks A-D
extend campus vocabulary	• Speaking • Task B
use different note-taking formats	• Reading 1 • Pre-text activity
know skimming as a reading technique	• Reading 1 • Task A
know referencing and bibliography	• Reading 1 • Task B
understand key words — significant words from a title or a document used especially as an index to content	• Reading 1 • Task C
debate on selected topics	• Reading 1 • Task D
have some knowledge of TED Talks	• Reading 2 • Pre-text activity
identify the author's attitude	• Reading 2 • Task A
recognize verb forms for hypothesizing and speculating	• Reading 2 • Task B
use expressions for suggesting, accepting and rejecting ideas	• Reading 2 • Task C
discuss with others about your reflection on the viewpoints of the text	• Reading 2 • Task D

SPEAKING

Task A | Orientation to Higher Education

Consider some issues regarding higher education in the US.
In recent years, the higher education in the United States has faced increasingly powerful challenges, and domestic criticism of the American university system has increased and become more intense.

1. Ask your partner the following questions:
    1) Do you know anything concerning higher education?
    2) What's the quantitative trend of graduates in your country?
    3) Compare the quantitative trend of graduates in your country with that in the United States.
    4) Will you further your postgraduate study abroad?
    5) Which country is your dreamed university located in?
    6) Should higher education be available to all students with sufficient academic ability? Why/Why not?
    7) Who should pay for higher education? The students themselves? Parents? Governments?
    8) Which subjects might you choose in higher education, and why?
        - vocational subjects, such as law or accounting
        - arts subjects, such as history or painting
        - pure science subjects, such as mathematics or medicine

2. Within a group discussion, please take notes on other students' ideas of the above questions by completing the table below.

Listing main ideas	Giving reasons or details

Task B | Extending Campus Vocabulary

1. In pairs, look at each set of the words below and try to decide whether they are the same or different. If different, what is the difference? You may use a learner's dictionary to help you understand it better.

   [a] campus/college/university/ normal university/branch school/ school of ...
   [b] department/office/faculty/ institute/academy
   [c] president/dean/professor/ associate professor/lecturer/ assistant/counselor/teaching secretary
   [d] applied science/pure science
   [e] philosophy/arts/humanities/law/ education/biology/political science/sociology/system science/economics/international relations/computer science/ electrical engineering
   [f] lecture/course/program/subject/ major/minor
   [g] quiz/essay/paper/presentation/ project/report/dissertation
   [h] midterm or final test/ attendance/participation/make-up examination/exam
   [i] compulsory or required courses/ prerequisite subject/optional or selective course
   [j] semester/term/trimester/seminar/ internship/tuition
   [k] academic performance/credit/score/ mark/GPA/transcript/certificate
   [l] third, lower second, upper second, first class/fail/pass/average/above average/distinction/high distinction/ excellent/scholarship
   [m] College Entrance Examination/ Entrance Examination of Master's Degree/IELTS/TOEFL/GRE
   [n] be admitted by some university/get registered/get enrolled
   [o] diploma/Bachelor/Honors/Master's degree/MBA/Professional Doctorate/ PhD
   [p] alumni/alumnus/alumna/Alumni Foundation

2. Discuss with your partner concerning higher education system by using the vocabulary from Question 1 to guide your discussion, and make notes on what you are going to talk about if necessary.
   1) Tell anything you know about your own country's higher education circumstance.
   2) Tell anything you know about the US higher education circumstance.
   3) Do you know the differences between education system in the US and that in your own country?

Listing your main ideas	Giving reasons or details

Reading 1

Pre-reading activity

1. With a partner or in groups, discuss the following questions:
   1) What social aspects do you think can influence higher education in your own country?
   2) List as many kinds of challenges of higher education as you can.
   3) For each, give an example to support your argument.
2. Here, look at the following **note formats**, try to choose one to guide your discussion.
   A. Spider Diagram / Mind Map

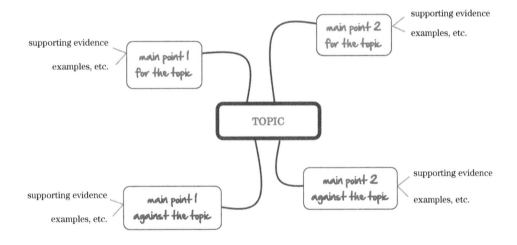

B. Table

Topic	
main point 1	supporting evidence 1 for main point 1
	supporting evidence 2 for main point 1
main point 2	supporting evidence 1 for main point 2
	supporting evidence 2 for main point 2
etc.	etc.

C. The Cornell Note-Taking System

Topic	Date
main point 1 for the topic	details (1) supporting evidence 1 for main point 1 (2) supporting evidence 2 for main point 1 (3) examples, data, etc.
main point 2 for the topic	(1) supporting evidence 1 for main point 2 (2) supporting evidence 2 for main point 2 (3) examples, data, etc.
main point 3 for the topic	(1) supporting evidence 1 for main point 3 (2) supporting evidence 2 for main point 3 (3) examples, data, etc.
points against the topic	(1) supporting evidence 1 for points against the topic (2) supporting evidence 2 for points against the topic (3) examples, data, etc.
Summary	

3. Which note-taking format mentioned above have you:
   ✓ used before?
   ✓ seen before but never used?
   ✓ never seen before?

4. Which note-taking format mentioned above do you think will be:
   • the easiest to use?
   • the most difficult to use?

5. Would it help you to take notes effectively by using those types of note formats?
   _____
   _____

The text you will read on the next page is an article from an online journal *Education News*. Read the text "US Higher Education Challenges", find five key challenges and solutions that American higher education is facing, and write them on the at the end of it.

Minutes
also known as protocols or notes
(as a summary or recommendation)

US Higher Education Challenges

Jan 1, 2020

Wafa Hozien, Ph.D Senior Contributor

EducationViews.org

[1] US Higher Education is facing a myriad of challenges and they impact all aspects of education. Keeping up with changing trends and the increasing demands of students, the workforce, the government has always been a priority in Higher Education (Pazzanese, 2017). Higher Education largely relies on traditional models and there is a widespread recognition that change may be beneficial, so they can fulfill their role in society. Below are the five most pressing challenges facing US Higher Education today and five possible solutions.

Increasing Enrollment

[2] There have been studies that show that many universities are failing to meet their enrollment goals (DMI Daily Digest, 2018). There are a number of reasons for this, they include the fact that many young people believe that universities are out of touch with the real world. Increasingly, universities are becoming more selective with regard to applications. Moreover, many minorities feel that they are going to be marginalized in Higher Education.

Solution

[3] Higher Education can streamline its application process to encourage more applicants. What we know is that application fees are a deterrent and not all students perform well on standardized test scores. Enter into the equation that admissions committees are just beginning to realize this. Some larger universities like the University of Maryland are not including application fees, SAT and GRE scores to lure students to their institutions. Game changer? Yes, indeed. Colleges and universities can engage in outreach programs to

appeal to minorities. Native Americans, African Americans and Latinos are still underrepresented in Higher Education, and they offer opportunities for universities to increase their student numbers. It is recommended that they demonstrate that they are relevant and can make a real difference in the outcomes of students.

Rising Costs

[4] The cost of Higher Education has been increasing in recent years and this is related to the growing privatization of education in America. This has led to the current crisis in student debt (Wiley Education Services, 2017). As a result, students are struggling to pay for their education and many universities are not adequately funded.

Solution

[5] Higher Education should look to reduce costs. This can be done by more flexible learning and the use of online teaching to limit costs (Zusman, 2005). Educators could seek to secure more investment from the private sector to replace government funding.

International Students

[6] Increasingly the US Higher Education sector is reliant on international students for enrollment and they are an important revenue stream. However, there is a challenge in attracting and retaining international students. This is because many American universities are falling in the World Ranking tables. Recent changes to the student visa program mean that there may be fewer international students able to enroll in the future in American universities (Zusman, 2005).

Solution

[7] It is important to make a university appealing to international students and to develop programs that can support their learning goals. It is not advisable for a university to become reliant on a small number of countries and it may be prudent to recruit students from a wide geographical area. It is also important that the Third Level sector should lobby against restrictions on student visas.

International students are not only good for Higher Education but also for the economy.

Declining Retention
⁸ One of the most disturbing trends in recent years are the abysmal graduation rates (DMI Daily Digest, 2018). More and more students are failing to complete their degrees. This results from high student debt with nothing to show for it. Then many students take many years to complete a degree, up to six to eight years and this is much higher than the international average.

Solution
⁹ This is a complex issue and one of the reasons for the low completion rates is the high costs. Students are working 2-3 jobs just to pay for their education, so they are enrolling in one semester and working for the next two semesters just to pay for college. More financial supports and flexible learning could help more students to complete their education. It is recommended that there is a system for early intervention with regard to students who are struggling with their workload or adjust to life on campus. Competency-based education could be a solution. This approach allows students to demonstrate their skills and competencies in a non-traditional way. Competency-based education is popular with many students and is particularly suited to adult learners.

On Campus Life
¹⁰ Research in American universities is increasingly dependent on commercial organizations and as a result, some research areas are not getting the support required. This has raised questions with regard to the relationship between education and industry. Then there are issues such as maintaining a balance between free speech and security (Press & Washburn, 2017). Since the "Me Too" movement began there is a growing concern about sexual violence and harassment on campus.

Solution
¹¹ Every university can continue to be a center for free expression and one

that provides everyone with a safe environment. It is important to collaborate with key stakeholders and businesses, but it is recommended that is at the expense of traditional academic pursuits. Higher Education should consider introducing policies to create an inclusive environment where difference is celebrated. Then it is essential that mechanisms are put in place to report sexual violence and harassment.

Key words: Higher Education, colleges, universities, student debt, graduation rates, retention rates, Higher Education funding, international students, Higher Education enrollment

Source: Hozien, W. (2020, January 1). US Higher Education challenges. *Education News*. Retrieved February 17, 2020, from https://www.educationviews.org/us-higher-education-challenges/.

References

DMI Daily Digest. (2018). 5 key challenges facing US Higher Education. *DMI*. <http://digitalmarketinginstitute.com/en-us/blog/5-key-challenges-facing-us-higher-education>

Pazzanese, C. (2017). The challenges facing Higher Education. *The Harvard Gazette*.

Press, E. & Washburn, J. (2017). *Academic Ethics*. London: Routledge.

Wiley Education Services. (2017). Top challenges facing US. *Higher Education*. <http://edservices.wiley.com/top-higher-education-challenges/>

Zusman, A. (2005). Challenges facing Higher Education in the twenty-first century. *American Higher Education in the Twenty-First Century: Social, Political, and Economic Challenges*, 2, 115–160. <http://www.educationanddemocracy.org/Resources/Zusman.pdf>

Minutes

Key Challenges	Solutions
- Challenge 1	- Solution 1
- Challenge 2	- Solution 2
- Challenge 3	- Solution 3
- Challenge 4	- Solution 4
- Challenge 5	- Solution 5

Post-reading activity

Task A | Reading Comprehension Strategy: Skimming for general ideas

1. Please identify the issues from the first paragraph of the above text and answer the questions in the following:

   1) From the introductory paragraph, can you say approximately how many challenges the author will talk about in the text?

   2) According to the author, is the student enrollment declining or increasing? How do you understand this trend?

   3) What is the reason for the student debt?

   4) Why is it called a challenge to attract and retain international students?

   5) There are several important ideas and solutions introduced in this text. What's your opinion of these solutions? Are these solutions effective for the mentioned challenges?

> ✓ ***Tips:***
> The best reading technique is to ...
> - read the whole article in order, word by word, sentence by sentence
> - read the first and last sentences of each paragraph, missing out the bits in between
> - do fast reading, only paying close attention to numbers, capital words, proper nouns ...
>
> Which of the reading techniques in the ***minutes*** and Question 1 did you practice respectively in Reading 1? What are they called?

> ✓ ***Skimming***
>
> Skimming, also called **reading for gist**, is a reading technique. It is reading an article quickly to get a general idea of meaning. If someone asks you to read just for the main ideas, skimming will help you do this. It can be contrasted with scanning, which is reading in order to find specific information, e.g. figures or names. (Find more on website: https://www.teachingenglish.org.uk/article/skimming)
>
> You will read a lot of English materials at university—maybe your professor will give you a long reading list in his/her module in each term. It is impossible to read word by word. So the question for you is how to read effectively and actively in a limited period of time. You can use skimming when you first read the article, in order to get its main idea, or help you identify whether the material is useful for your group task, or find the most crucial parts in an article for intensive reading (eg. common in reading academic materials, newspaper, e-mails, or even in an exam).
>
> When you do skimming, you can pay attention to the following information
> → titles and sub-headings
> → introduction
> → the beginning and end of a paragraph, where topic sentence is often found
> → headlines and captions of pictures, graphs, etc.
> → capitalized words, or words in **bold** or *italics*

2. Differences between ***skimming, scanning,*** and ***intensive reading***

   The table below shows the features of **skimming, scanning, and intensive** reading. Work in groups, tick the best reading technique(s) for them. More than one answer is possible to choose.

This reading technique	SKIMMING ✓	SCANNING ✓	INTENSIVE READING ✓
[a] ... is the same with fast reading			
[b] ... helps you get the main idea/the gist of a text			
[c] ... helps you efficiently get the particular piece of information you need		✓	
[d] ... needs more time than the others			✓
[e] ... helps you grasp the author's attitude of the text			
[f] ... requires a careful reading in one sentence or in one paragraph			
To use the technique, you need to			
[g] ... read or look at something quickly without looking at the details	✓		
[h] ... read the first and last paragraph of a text, or read the first and last sentence of each paragraph of a text			
[i] ... skip the words or phrases you don't understand			
[j] ... look for specific information, such as numbers, dates, etc.			
[k] ... read each word in one paragraph			
[l] ... understand each word, number or fact			
[m] ... look for main ideas only			
[n] ... search for key words or ideas you need			
[o] ... focus on topic sentences, summary sentences, introductions, and conclusions			
[p] ... do less reading and more searching			
By using the technique, you can			
[q] ... understand the structure of the text			
[r] ... understand a text thoroughly			
[s] ... read accurately for detailed understanding			

3. Skimming race
   Read the question first. Then skim the text "US Higher Education Challenges". Put your hand up and answer the question when you finish.
   Which one is the text structure?
   1) introduction → facts → problems → reasons → solutions
   2) introduction → problems → facts → reasons → solutions
   3) introduction → reasons → facts → problems → solutions

Task B | Language Spotlight: Referencing and bibliography

You may recognize the following references. They are from Reading 1 "US Higher Education Challenges".

References
[1] DMI Daily Digest. (2018). 5 key challenges facing US Higher Education. *DMI*. < http://digitalmarketinginstitute. com/en-us/blog/5-key-challenges-facing-us-higher-education >
[2] Pazzanese, C. (2017). The challenges facing Higher Education. *The Harvard Gazette*.
[3] Press, E. & Washburn, J. (2017). *Academic Ethics*. London: Routledge.
[4] Wiley Education Services. (2017). Top challenges facing US. *Higher Education*. < http://edservices. wiley. com/top-higher-education-challenges/ >
[5] Zusman, A. (2005). Challenges facing Higher Education in the twenty-first century. *American Higher Education in the Twenty-First Century: Social, Political, and Economic Challenges*, 2, 115–160. < http://www. educationanddemocracy. org/Resources/Zusman. pdf >

Referencing & Bibliography

When you read an academic article, you will find that there is a reference list in the end of the text, just like the above reference list of Reading 1. Referencing usually refers to the source of the content you quote directly or indirectly in a paper or article. In college, you have the opportunity to write academic papers as the assignments of specific courses. Writing academic papers requires you to read a lot of reference books, and you may refer the information in your own writing from these reading materials. All the pieces of information you cite are called references. Referencing could make your views more convincing.

And bibliography usually refers to the referenced books that have been referenced during the writing process, and some of them are not actually cited in your paper. You were inspired by the referenced books, and reading of these books is also for the preparation of this paper.

Referencing is a must! Not listed or not fully listed references may constitute the crime of plagiarism, which means you have "stolen" others' thoughts but haven't told the reader. And in Western universities, your professor will give you a "FAIL".

1. How is the article (Reading 1) referenced?
   Discuss with your partner, and answer the questions in the table.

Questions	Answers
① Identify the reference provided for *many universities are failing to meet their enrollment goals.*	
② Identify the reference of *the situation of student debt.*	
③ What year did Pazzanese write the information referenced?	
④ Are the titles of books *italicized* in the reference list?	
⑤ How are the names of the authors organized and presented within this list of references?	
⑥ How are the initials of the authors organized and presented in the reference list?	
⑦ How should you present the dates of publication in the reference list?	
⑧ In reference [5], what do the numbers "2, 115–160" represent respectively?	
⑨ What are the volume numbers? And how are the volume numbers presented in the reference list?	
⑩ How to cite references within the text	

2. Referencing from the Internet

When writing a paper, if you want to cite some articles from the Internet (the electronic document), how should you put them in the references correctly? Examine the references on Page 38 and answer the following questions:

1) What does http:// mean?
   [a] a travelling magazine
   [b] a book
   [c] a website

2) Is http:// and the following information a URL?
   [a] Yes
   [b] No

3) Identify the **news source** of **Reading 1**.

> DMI Daily Digest. (2018). 5 key challenges facing US Higher Education. *DMI*. <http://digitalmarketinginstitute.com/en-us/blog/5-key-challenges-facing-us-higher-education>

4) Identify the **news source** of the **fourth** reference of **Reading 1**.

> Wiley Education Services. (2017). Top challenges facing US. *Higher Education*. <http://edservices.wiley.com/top-higher-education-challenges/>

3. Citation patterns

Look at the explanations for citation patterns in the table below. And finish the following related exercise.

Citation Patterns

Citation Patterns	Definitions
Quotations	Quotations must be the same as the original, using a short segment of the source. They must match the source document verbatim, and the original author must be noted.
Paraphrasing	Paraphrasing involves putting a paragraph from the original material into your own words. Paraphrasing must also indicate the original source. The paraphrased material is usually shorter than the original paragraph, summarizing its meaning and slightly condensed.
Summarizing	Summarizing involves expressing the main ideas in your own words, including only the main points. It is necessary to indicate the original source. The summary is much shorter than the original material and provides an extensive overview of the source material.

Examine the references on Page 38 and tick the right citation patterns:

Order	Name and date	Paragraph	Quotation	Paraphrase
1	Zusman, 2005	5 & 6		√
2	Press, E. & Washburn, J., 2017			
3	Pazzanese, C. (2017)			
4	DMI Daily Digest. (2018)			

4. Evaluating the credibility of Internet resources

Credibility

n. the quality of being believed or accepted as true, real or honest (*Merriam-Webster, the English Language Learners Dictionary*)

Is the information on the Internet reliable? If you decide to use the Internet resource in your paper, what factors would you consider to judge its reliability? Discuss which types of websites are credible enough for further information investigation.

Listing your main ideas	Giving reasons or details

Task C | Vocabulary Practice: Understanding key words

1. Words describing trends

   In Reading 1, there are a lot of words describing trends.

   1) What do the following words mean? Put them in the correct column in the table below.

   - increase
   - fall
   - decrease
   - reduce
   - rise
   - grow
   - decline
   - drop
   - climb
   - jump

GO UP ↗	GO DOWN ↘

   2) Using your shared knowledge or a dictionary, decide which of the words in the table:

   ✓ Have the same form as a noun and as a verb

✓ Can be changed from a verb to a noun by removing the last letter and adding "-ion"

Notes	

2. Key words
   1) Look for and underline the key words in the reading text "US Higher Education Challenges".
   2) Match the words or phrases in the first column to the definition in the second column and write the number of the word in front of the definition in the table. You should be able to determine their meaning from the context within the text.

Key words
a significant word from a title or document used especially as an index to content
——Merriam Webster

KEY WORDS	DEFINITIONS
i. a myriad of	A _____ a great deal of; a large amount of
ii. impact	B _____ compelling immediate action
iii. beneficial	C _____ make a group of people feel isolated and unimportant
iv. pressing	D _____ advantageous; healthful
v. marginalize	E _____ immeasurably low or wretched; extremely poor or bad
vi. abysmal	F _____ uninvited and unwelcome verbal or physical behavior of a sexual nature especially by a person in authority toward a subordinate (such as an employee or student)
vii. sexual harassment	G _____ everything around us
viii. environment	H _____ influence; effect; outcome
ix. retention rate	I _____ the total number of students properly registered and/or attending classes at a school
x. enrollment	J _____ an important gauge of any educational institution's success; it indicates the percentage of students who remain at an educational institution after they begin studying there
xi. student debt	K _____ a form of debt that is owed by an attending, withdrawn or graduated student to a lending institution

In the last part of Reading 1 "*On Campus Life*", there are key words of "**MeToo**" **movement, sexual violence and harassment**. Do you know the exact meanings of them?

Let's read the word notes below, and you will also have an opportunity to discuss recent changes brought about by #METoo movement.

#MeToo Movement

It is an online campaign against sexual harassment and sexual assault. Victims are encouraged to tell their own experiences and try to arouse people's attention to sexual harassment and sexual assault.

The hashtag "MeToo" appeared on social media in 2017 in response to a number of high-profile sexual assault allegations in the entertainment industry. It quickly spread to other societal domains and continues to spur discussion and action around the world.

Find more on website: https://www.coursera.org/lecture/feminism-social-justice/metoo-NpCeP

Sexual Violence and Harassment

Young people have always been targeted for sexual abuse and exploitation by adults and by one another. As a society we have sometimes ignored the harm sexual violence and sexual harassment can cause.

Sexual violence is rape, assault by penetration or sexual assault. Sexual harassment is unwanted conduct of a sexual nature. Harmful sexual behaviour is problematic, abusive and violent behaviour that is developmentally inappropriate and may cause developmental damage.

Find more on website: Safeguarding Network https://safeguarding.network/

Listing your main ideas	Giving reasons or details
	Reason 1 -
	Supporting evidence:
	Reason 2 -
	Supporting evidence:
	Reason 3 -
	Supporting evidence:
Summary	

Task D | Critical Thinking: Debate on selected topics!

Critical Thinking is a mode of thinking, which is a way for a person to see the world or an attitude towards academics.

The ancient Greek sage Socrates advocated an inquiry-based questioning, asking the students to clarify the purpose of their thinking or research and their meaning through questions and rebuttals, distinguishing relevant and irrelevant information, testing its reliability and source, and questioning the assumptions said by themselves and others.

In the 19th century, the British politician Edmond Burke expressed the same point: Reading without reflection is like eating without digestion.

The person who really established the model of modern science critical thinking is John Dewey, a well-known American psychologist, philosopher, educator, and pragmatist master. Dewey proposed "reflective thinking"—an exploratory model of critical thinking.

Debate

1. Do you think that Higher Education is facing the challenges outlined in this article?
2. Why? Or why not?
3. What else do you think are possible solutions to these ongoing issues in Higher Education?

Yes	No
Reason 1 - Supporting evidence : Reason 2 - Supporting evidence : Reason 3 - Supporting evidence : Solutions:	Reason 1 - Supporting evidence : Reason 2 - Supporting evidence : Reason 3 - Supporting evidence : Solutions:

Reading 2

Pre-reading activity

Reading 2 is the excerpts from a public talk script, which is retrieved from TED Talks website. This talk was presented at an official TED conference, and was featured by TED editors on the home page. Let's grab some knowledge of TED Talks first.

TED Ideas worth spreading

> TED is a nonprofit organization devoted to spreading ideas, usually in the form of short, powerful talks (18 minutes or less). TED began in 1984 as a conference where Technology, Entertainment and Design converged, and today covers almost all topics—from science to business to global issues—in more than 100 languages. Meanwhile, independently run TEDx events help share ideas in communities around the world.
>
> —Find more on website https://www.ted.com

1. Have you ever logged on to the TED Talks website to watch a talk?
2. If yes, what kind of topics of public talks did you watch on TED Talks?
3. Discuss with your partner, share your TED Talks experiences with them.

TED Talks you have watched	No
	Please take notes of the main points of the public talks that other students have watched on the TED Talks.

The Child-Driven Education
— "Hole in the Wall" Experiments
Sugata Mitra
TEDGlobal 2010 July 2010

About the speaker

Sugata Mitra · Education researcher
Educational researcher Sugata Mitra is the winner of the 2013 TED Prize. His wish: Build a School in the Cloud, where children can explore and learn from one another.

In 1999, Sugata Mitra and his colleagues dug a hole in a wall bordering an urban slum in New Delhi, installed an Internet-connected PC and left it there, with a hidden camera filming the area. What they saw: kids from the slum playing with the computer and, in the process, learning how to use it—then teaching each other. These famed "Hole in the Wall" experiments demonstrated that, in the absence of supervision and formal teaching, children can teach themselves and each other—if they're motivated by curiosity. Mitra, now a professor of educational technology at Newcastle University, called it "minimally invasive education".

Excerpts:

1 "If you think of a map of your country, I think you'll realize that for every country on Earth, you could draw little circles to say, 'These are places where good teachers won't go.' On top of that, those are the places from where trouble comes. We have an ironic problem: good teachers don't want to go to just those places where they're needed the most. I started in 1999 to try and address this problem with an experiment, which was a very simple experiment in New Delhi. I basically embedded a computer into a wall of a slum in New Delhi. The children barely went to school, they didn't know any English, they'd never seen a computer before, and they didn't know what the Internet was. I connected high speed Internet to it—it's about three feet off the ground, I turned it on and left it there. After this, we noticed a couple of interesting things, which you'll see. But I repeated this all over India and then through a large part of the world and noticed that children will learn to do what they want to learn to do."

2 "I think I can make a guess now education is a self-organizing system,

where learning is an emergent phenomenon. It'll take a few years to prove it, experimentally, but I'm going to try."

³ "This is the first experiment that we did: an eight-year-old boy on your right teaching his student, a six-year-old girl, and he was teaching her how to browse. This boy here in the middle of central India, a Rajasthan village, where the children recorded their own music and then played it back to each other and in the process, they've enjoyed themselves thoroughly. They did all of this in four hours after seeing the computer for the first time."

⁴ "So at the end of it, we concluded that groups of children can learn to use computers and the Internet on their own, irrespective of who or where they were."

⁵ "I got an interesting phone call once from Columbo, from the late Arthur C. Clarke (1917 – 2008), who said, 'I want to see what's going on.' He said two interesting things, 'A teacher that can be replaced by a machine.' The second thing he said was that, 'if children have interest, then education happens.' Arthur C. Clarke: '... and they can definitely help people, because children quickly learn to navigate the web and find things which interest them.' This is what I'm building now they're called SOLEs: Self-Organized Learning Environments."

Mitra thinks self-organized learning will shape the future of education. At TED2013, he made a bold TED Prize wish: Help me build a School in the Cloud where children can explore and learn on their own—and teach one another—using resources from the worldwide cloud.

The School in the Cloud now includes seven physical locations—five in India and two in the UK. At the same time, the School in the Cloud online platform lets students participate anywhere, with partner learning labs and programs in countries like Colombia, Pakistan and Greece. In 2016, Mitra held the first School in the Cloud conference in India. He shared that more than 16,000 SOLE sessions had taken place so far, with kids all around the world dipping their toes into this new education model.

Please go to this official website to see the full version of this TED Talk.

Source: Mitra, S. (2010, July). The child-driven education—"hole in the wall" experiments [Speech]. *TED*. Retrieved August 1, 2020, from https://www.ted.com/talks/sugata_mitra_the_child_driven_education? language = zh-cn.

Post-reading activity

Task A | Reading Comprehension Strategy: Identifying the author's attitude

Attitude

Attitude includes any way of expressing feelings or emotions toward a subject or a fact. Attitude can be presented through the choice of words or intonation. For example, if someone feels negative or hostile about something, he/she can perform a cool, or arrogant manner with negative adjectives, and he/she may say it in a strong tone. If someone is not certain about something, he/she can use words such as "perhaps", and he/she can also use an ascending or questioning tone. Generally speaking, ascending intonation shows uncertainty, and falling intonation shows certainty.

- Read the excerpts again.
1. Mark the words that the speaker talks with his attitude about poor education.
2. Then compare your answers with another student's.
3. Did the speaker use words, intonation or both to convey his attitude?

Attitude: *certain*, *negative*, *sad*, *hostile*, *aggressive*, *positive*, *conservative*, *humorous*, *unsure/ tentative*, *etc.*

Discussion

Points from the TED Talks excerpts	In comparison with others' answers

Task B | Language Spotlight: Verb forms for hypothesizing and speculating

1. Look at the following examples from the TED Talks in Reading 2. With a partner, answer the questions.

   [i] If children have interest, then education happens.

   [ii] I think I can make a guess now education is a self-organizing system, where learning is an emergent phenomenon. It'll take a few years to prove it, experimentally, but I'm going to try.

   1) From your experience of English, which example—[i] or [ii]—feels the most hypothetical? Which feels more definite?

   2) Which verb form (or tense) expresses the great certainty of these examples? Complete the "IF" clause and main clause columns of the table below.

	Hypothetical/Speculative	
	"IF" clause	Main clause
simple present tense	simple present tense	will + verb
	e. g. If it <u>rains</u> tomorrow, we <u>will cancel</u> the picnic. Rewrite it as a declarative sentence →	
past time reference	simple past tense past perfect e. g.　were 　　　had done	would + verb would have + past participle
	e. g. If I <u>were</u> young, I <u>could</u> enjoy this party. (declarative sentence) → Because I am not young, I can't enjoy this party. If you <u>heard</u> him talk, you <u>would</u> <u>think</u> he <u>knew</u> all about the secret. → If I <u>had known</u> the gossip then, I <u>would</u> <u>have</u> <u>told</u> you. → If I <u>had done</u> my homework yesterday, I <u>would</u> <u>go</u> on a date with her now. →	

| | Hypothetical/Speculative ||
	"IF" clause	Main clause
present or future time reference	should + verb were to	would/will + verb
	e. g. If it <u>should rain</u> tomorrow, the game <u>would (will) be put off</u>. → If the Pacific Ocean <u>were to dry up</u>, I <u>would change</u> my mind. → I never change my mind. I <u>will stay</u> here <u>provided</u> the climate <u>agrees</u> with me tomorrow. →	

Note: "**would**" can be replaced by **could, may, might, should**, etc.
"**if**" can be replaced by **as if, as though, supposing, suppose (that), providing, provided**, etc.

Practice

2. Choose three topics you are interested in. Discuss them by using hypothesizing and speculating forms.

If true	If not true

Task C | Vocabulary Practice: Expressions for suggesting, accepting and rejecting ideas

Tutorial discussions

In the western university system, you will have the opportunity to participate in tutorials each semester. As we learned in Unit 1, the tutorial discussion may occur during tutorials or group seminars. Generally, an instructor and a group of students will participate together. The minimum number of participants may be about 10, and at most 50 or 60 may be involved. In a tutorial discussion, the instructor guides everyone to discuss what you've acquired in class or after-class thinking questions. You may get a corresponding score for participating in the tutorial discussion, so it is very crucial for you to contribute during discussion. In these discussions, you can come up with your own ideas, and strive to gain support in the discussion, or accept other students' proposals, or raise objections, and attach your reasons. In this section, you will practice some polite expressions about suggesting, accepting and rejecting ideas.

1. Match the correct expressions below with the appropriate classification on the right.
2. Add any other expressions you know and discuss with your partner.

Don't take this the wrong way ...
I hold the view that ...
I am convinced that ...
Shall we ...?
Why not do sth ...?
Will you please ...?
I'd like to suggest that ...
Well, personally, I'm in favor of this.
It's an excellent idea.
That's out of the question ...
I do agree with you that ...

| Suggesting an idea |

| Accepting an idea |

| Rejecting an idea |

Other expressions

Task D | Critical Thinking: Reflecting on the viewpoints of the text

1. Work in groups. Prepare a conversation, similar to a tutorial discussion in the previous task, which you can present to the whole class.
   1) Think about the question posted by the TED Talks speaker, the educational researcher Mitra. Do you agree or disagree with his hypothesis?
   2) How do you think of the scientific research achievements in Mitra's experiment?
   3) Compare with the educational situation in your own country. What are the educational problems in poor areas?
   4) Try to include as many pragmatic functions listed in the table below in your discussion as possible. You can use the "own group" column to guide your discussion.

Functions	Own group	Other groups
Expressing understanding, but partial agreement		
Raising a hypothetical or speculating idea		
Paying attention to the logic of your viewpoint (by using linking words)		
Supporting a viewpoint with examples and evidences		
Indicating a sufficient rebuttal and stating relevant supporting evidences and examples		
Linking back to a previous viewpoint		
Making a conclusion		

Note: When you present your conversation to other groups, your audience will tick off the functions in their table as they listen.

2. Discuss these questions:
   1) Which group uses the most pragmatic functions in the above list?
   2) Which group offers the most persuasive arguments? And why?
   3) Which way of presenting a viewpoint impresses you the most?

Notes

Glossary of Unit 2

Reading 1

myriad
n. 1. ten thousand
2. a great number
e.g. a <u>myriad</u> of ideas

keep up with
to go or make progress at the same rate as (others); to stay even with (others) in a race, competition, etc.
e.g. He found it difficult to <u>keep up with</u> the rest of the class.

trend
n. a general direction in which something tends to move
e.g. Economic <u>trends</u> are running counter to the forecasts.

workforce
n. the workers engaged in a specific activity or enterprise
e.g. A quarter of the local <u>workforce</u> is unemployed.

priority
n. earlier in time or order; taking precedence
e.g. The highest <u>priority</u> of governments has been given to the problem of heavy traffic.

recognition
n. the action of recognizing; the state of being recognized
e.g. My <u>recognition</u> of him was immediate.

beneficial
adj. producing good results or helpful effects
e.g. Sunshine is <u>beneficial</u> to plants.

enrollment
n. the process of initiating attendance to a school; the total number of students properly registered and/or attending classes at a school
e.g. The class has an <u>enrollment</u> of 27 students.

selective
adj. of, relating to, or characterized by selection; selecting or tending to select
e.g. She is <u>selective</u> about the clothes she buys.

minority
n. a group of people who differ racially or politically from a larger group of which it is a part
e.g. The white <u>minority</u> once ruled over South Africa.

deterrent
n. a thing that makes sb. less likely to do sth.
e.g. The fact that they believed Wall Street was "always doing this" was not a <u>deterrent</u>; it was a recommendation.

privatization
n. a state of change from public to private control or ownership
e.g. There were fears that <u>privatization</u> would lead to job losses.

struggle to/with
to continue doing sth. that is difficult or tiring

e. g. Not only have countries <u>struggled to</u> roll out wide-scale testing for the virus, those efforts inevitably will miss people who have recovered from an infection.

adequately

adv. to an adequate or sufficient degree or extent

e. g. There is no way to <u>adequately</u> prepare yourself for encountering a wild mountain gorilla.

flexible

adj. capable of being flexed

e. g. a <u>flexible</u> schedule

investment

n. the outlay of money usually for income or profit, capital outlay; also the sum invested or the property purchased

e. g. An <u>investment</u> is an asset intended to produce income or capital gains.

funding

n. an organization administering a special fund

e. g. initial <u>funding</u>

reliant

adj. having reliance on something or someone; dependent

e. g. The additional cases also threaten to disrupt shipments and delay deliveries even as millions of Americans are becoming more <u>reliant</u> on the service as they are told to leave their homes as little as possible.

revenue stream

It is a form of revenue. It is considered one of the building blocks of a business model canvas, that reveals the earning a business makes from all the methods by which money comes in.

e. g. A <u>revenue stream</u> is a way of categorizing the earnings a company makes.

retain

vt. to keep in possession or use; to keep in mind or memory

e. g. He <u>retained</u> the copyright of his book.

visa

n. an endorsement made on a passport by the proper authorities denoting that it has been examined and that the bearer may proceed

e. g. The couple was supposed to meet for a five-week trip in India in March, but canceled after Ariel was unable to secure a <u>visa</u>.

appeal

v. to attract or interest sb.

e. g. The large salary made their offer even more <u>appealing</u> to him.

prudent

adj. marked by wisdom or judiciousness

e. g. <u>prudent</u> advice

geographical

adj. 1. of or relating to geography

2. belonging to or characteristic of a particular region

e. g. the <u>geographical</u> features of Ohio

lobby

v. to try to influence a politician or the government and, for example, persuade them to support or oppose a change in the law

e. g. ... continued to <u>lobby</u> for American support of ...

disturbing

adj. causing feelings of worry, concern, or anxiety

e. g. <u>disturbing</u> news

retention rate

Student retention rate is an important gauge of any educational institution's success. It indicates the percentage of students who remain at an educational institution after they begin studying there.

e.g. A high retention rate suggests a school is supportive and enjoyable and that the workload is manageable.

Especially at the college and graduate level, retention rates play a vital role in attracting high quality students.

abysmal

adj. immeasurably low or wretched; extremely poor or bad

e.g. abysmal ignorance/poverty

recommend

v. 1. to present as worthy of acceptance or trial
2. to make acceptable
3. to suggest an act or course of action

e.g. There is much besides fishing to recommend a trip to this sleepy fishing village.

intervention

n. the act or an instance of intervening, such as the act of interfering with the outcome or course especially of a condition or process (as to prevent harm or improve functioning)

e.g. educational intervention

workload

n. 1. the amount of work or of working time expected or assigned

e.g. students with a heavy workload

2. the amount of work performed or capable of being performed (as by a mechanical device) usually within a specific period

e.g. Students complained about the heavy workload.

competency

n. possession of sufficient knowledge or skill; a specific area of competence

e.g. I have always believed businesses that concentrate on a very few core competencies will do the best. —Bill Gates

demonstrate

v. to show clearly

e.g. demonstrate a willingness to cooperate

commercial

adj. of or relating to commerce

e.g. commercial regulations

sexual violence

It is any sexual act or attempt to obtain a sexual act by violence or coercion, unwanted sexual comments or advances, acts to traffic a person or acts directed against a person's sexuality, regardless of the relationship to the victim.

harassment

n. annoying or unpleasant behaviour towards someone that takes place regularly, for example, threats, offensive remarks, or physical attacks, especially by uninvited and unwelcome verbal or physical conduct

e.g. We take every case of harassment seriously and will stand against it as we stand against the breaking of every human right.

collaborate

v. to work jointly with others or together especially in an intellectual endeavor

e.g. An international team of scientists collaborated on the study.

stakeholder

n. one that has a stake in an enterprise

e.g. Others hope that the present challenge will also open to more intense and multilateral and multi-stakeholder corporations.

at the expense of

in a way that harms (something or someone)

e. g. He argues that the tax cut will benefit the rich at the expense of the poor.

pursuit

n. 1. the act of pursuing

2. an activity that one engages in as a vocation, profession, or avocation

e. g. She enjoys reading, knitting, and other quiet pursuits.

inclusive

adj. 1. broad in orientation or scope

2. covering or intended to cover all items, costs, or services

3. including everyone

e. g. The industry and our country are changing and wisely becoming more inclusive and strategic in reaching new segments and diverse communities.

mechanism

n. a method or process for getting something done within a system or organization

e. g. new management mechanisms

dig

v. 1. to bring to the surface by digging

2. to turn up, loosen, or remove earth

e. g. digging in the garden

slum

n. a densely populated urban area marked by crowding, run-down housing, poverty, and social disorganization

e. g. He grew up in the slums of New York.

install

v. to set up for use or service

e. g. install software

famed

adj. famous; very well known; known by many people for a particular quality or achievement

e. g. the famed White Cliffs of Dove

motivate

v. to provide with a motive

e. g. She was motivated by a desire to help children.

curiosity

n. the desire to know

e. g. Her natural curiosity led her to ask more questions.

minimally

adv. relating to or being a minimum

e. g. minimally invasion

invasive

adj. tending to spread especially in a quick or aggressive manner

e. g. invasive infection

ironic

adj. given to irony

e. g. an ironic sense of humor

embed

v. to fix or set securely or deeply; to insert (a media file, such as a graphic, video, or audio clip) into a computer document

e. g. The arrow embedded itself in the wall.

The company lets users embed video and audio attachments in E-mail messages.

barely

adv. scarcely, hardly

e. g. barely enough money for lunch

emergent

adj. appearing, arising, occurring, or developing, especially for the first time

e. g. Emergent behavior exists in many natural, social and other complex systems.

browse

v. to scan and view files in a computer database or on the Internet, especially on the World Wide Web

e. g. browse and upload for picture and videos

irrespective

adj. lacking in respect

e. g. It must be done, irrespective of cost.

navigate

v. to move between the different areas of a website by using the links provided in it

e. g. navigate website

dip one's toes into

also, get one's toes into or wet, get one's feet wet begin to do sth. novel or unfamiliar

e. g. I have been dipping my toes into Asian cooking.

US Colleges Fret Over Fall in Chinese Students

By Lia Zhu in San Francisco | *China Daily* | Updated: 2019-03-06 07:45

Decline in new enrollments leads to budget cuts

Nearly 1.1 million international students are studying at universities and colleges in the United States, contributing $42 billion to the country's economy. For every seven international students enrolled, three US jobs are created and supported through tuition and other expenses.

However, the years of easy growth may be over for many of the schools as new enrollment of international students has declined for a third consecutive year.

New student enrollments fell from the 2016–2017 academic year by 6.6 percent for the 2017–2018 period, according to a new study.

Chinese students take part in a graduation ceremony at Columbia University in New York last year. Guo Ke/Xinhua

However, overall—as opposed to new—international enrollments increased by 1.5 percent from 2016 – 2017 to 2017 – 2018, according to a survey last year by the Institute of International Education in New York. It collected data from 2,075 institutions.

The report also found that most of the international students are from China, with more than 363,000 enrolling in the 2017 – 2018 school year, or about one-third of the total international student population in the US.

Several states, including Arkansas, Montana and Tennessee, saw their international student numbers decline by double digits.

The universities of Illinois, Oregon and Iowa reported enrollment declines among international students for the fall last year, especially from China, the largest contributor to the US.

Rahul Choudaha, research associate at the Center for Studies in Higher Education at the University of California, Berkeley, said the loss of Chinese students, who often pay higher tuition rates, would be financially catastrophic for US universities.

As an example, he cited Michigan State University, which enrolled 486 fewer undergraduate students from China in the fall semester last year.

Based on the university's annual $40,000 international undergraduate tuition fee, 486 fewer students means a loss of nearly $20 million in revenue in the first year and $80 million in four years, Choudaha said.

"Public universities are even more dependent on international students, especially those from China, because of the decline in domestic enrollment and the government's budgetary support," he said.

At UC Berkeley, China provides the largest number of foreign students, accounting for more than 37 percent of the international total. In the fall, the university had 2,448 Chinese students, 169 more than at the same time the previous year, a rise of 7.42 percent. Tuition and fees for international undergraduates are $46,170 a year, according to the university's international office.

The fall in international enrollments has led to budget cuts at some institutions. Wright State University in Ohio has reduced the number of full-time French horn and tuba professors, and Kansas State University has reduced its Italian classes, according to media reports.

Two colleges at the University of Illinois have insured themselves against a sharp drop in the number of Chinese students, to manage financial risks to their programs.

Jeffrey Brown, dean of the university's business college, came up with the idea in 2015, when international enrollments were high.

In 2017, Brown's college and the engineering college agreed to pay $424,000 annually for insurance coverage of up to $60 million—about the combined annual tuition revenue from the 800 Chinese students at the two colleges.

Kevin Pitts, vice-provost for undergraduate education at the university, said about one in seven of its undergraduates are international, out of a student body of about 33,000, and China is the biggest contributor to international enrollments.

He said the direct cause of the fall in international students is unknown, but there are several potential reasons.

"Educators and schools in China could be increasing their capacity to cater to domestic students. Another thing we wonder about in this political climate is the availability of visas," Pitts said.

"Visa application process issues or visa delays/denials" is listed as the top reason for reduced new enrollment in the fall last year, according to the Institute of International Education.

Its Fall 2018 International Student Enrollment Hot Topics Survey found that 83 percent of the respondents attributed the decline in numbers to visa delays and denials, compared with 34 percent in the fall of 2016.

Although the factors causing these declines are likely to be multifaceted, the "Trump effect" stands out clearly, said Choudaha, the research associate at UC Berkeley also executive vice-president at Studyportals, a company that recruits international students online.

A ban on visitors from some Muslim countries initially put forward by the administration of US President Donald Trump, and a proposed ban on all Chinese students going to the US, which were later dropped, have created perceptions of the country becoming unattractive and unsafe for international students, Choudaha said.

Nicole Shen, from Suzhou, Jiangsu province, said she is considering the University of Toronto in Canada for her daughter, who is attending a high school in Palo Alto, California.

"Canada is more welcoming, and it has better immigration policies. I heard it's easier to get a work visa after graduation. And if you work for three consecutive years, you can get a green card (permanent residency)," she said.

Safety and a perceived anti-immigration climate are her only concerns. "Money is not a worry," Shen said. "We would rather sell property to support our child." The family has a budget of $50,000 for annual college tuition fees.

According to a survey in 2017 by Studyportals, a company in Boston that offers an online international student recruitment platform, nearly two-thirds of 1,815 prospective students said they would lose interest in studying in the US due to changes that limit work opportunities for students from abroad.

Choudaha said in a report on international student mobility published by UC Berkeley in April that the ability to work while a student, and paths to entering the US job market and possibly becoming a citizen, are also critical factors for many students selecting their foreign study destinations.

Overseas students are experiencing more visa issues in the US when they apply to stay and work.

Min Yuhan, a Chinese student at Foothill College in the Bay Area, California, said, "I know many graduates have been turned down by Silicon Valley companies. Compared with a few years ago, the situation is worse now."

The college Min attends has 1,621 international students. "Every year, we have more than 100 new students from China," he said.

The increasing popularity of community colleges among Chinese students has prompted Min to launch a startup providing a "one-stop" service for such students to study at these institutions in the US.

Min, who has a company in Hangzhou, Zhejiang Province, said, "The decisions are mostly made by parents. Aside from the safety issues, visa hassles and slim hopes of landing a job are cooling interest in Chinese sending their children to America."

Elizabeth Venturini, a college admissions consultant in California, said, "With studies for a four-year college degree costing anywhere from $150,000 to $260,000, parents can not afford to make a financial mistake with their child's education."

The main reasons for Chinese families sending their children to the US are to avoid the stress of taking the gaokao—the national college entrance exam—and to learn or improve their English-speaking skills, Venturini said.

An increasing number of options are available to meet such demands. Australia, Canada and the United Kingdom are the biggest competitors to the US, she said.

Some of the world's top international student hosting countries have seen growing enrollment due to official recruitment efforts.

In 2016, Australia launched its National Strategy for International Education 2025 to develop the country's role as a global leader in education and research.

As a result, the number of international students in the country reached a record high in 2017, with more than 690,000 enrolled for the fall semester last year, according to the Australian Department of Education and Training.

Canada has also taken measures to invite international students to the country as part of a government strategy to attract talent for job creation and economic growth. The country's efforts include quickly processing student visas and creating pathways for certain international students to remain in Canada after graduation.

Canada has seen a steady increase in international enrollment since 2014. There were nearly 500,000 international students in the country in 2017, a 17 percent year-on-year increase, according to a report by the Canadian Bureau for International Education in August.

Choudaha said in his report, "American Higher Education is entering a new era of intensified competition. Institutions must identify ways to reinvest some of the income generated by international student tuition toward proactive outreach strategies and creative scholarship packages that broaden and diversify the pool of prospective international students. "

Source: Zhu, L. (2019, March 6). US colleges fret over fall in Chinese students. *China Daily*. Retrieved August 10, 2020, from http://www.chinadaily.com.cn/kindle/2019-03/06/content_37444677.htm.

Unit 3

Love and Friendship

Friendship is love without wings. —*George G. Byron*, **British poet**
Friendship may, and often does, grow in love, but love never subsides into friendship. —*George G. Byron*, **British poet**

I think love is of all passions the strongest, for it attacks simultaneously the head, the heart and the senses.
I think that friendship is the basic need of human feeling.
What do you think about love and friendship?

In this unit, you will have a look at issues about love and friendship and examine the differences between love and friendship. You will practice reading strategies of skimming for gist and summarizing. Also, you will learn about language and lexical features that are typically used in an academic context and will practice using them appropriately.

English Reading for Academic Purposes 1A

By the end of this unit, you will be able to:	
SKILL	TASK
skim a passage efficiently to get general ideas	• Reading 1 • Task A
use appropriate language to refer to sources	• Reading 1 • Task B
use hyphenated words correctly	• Reading 1 • Task C
do critical thinking on love and friendship on campus	• Reading 1 • Task D
summarize ideas in a text	• Reading 2 • Task A
use language for contrasts	• Reading 2 • Task B
correctly use verbs related to giving definitions	• Reading 2 • Task C
do critical thinking on differences between platonic and romantic love	• Reading 2 • Task D

Reading 1

We All Need Friends

1 We all know college is a formative time in a person's life. While we're moving through this important time in our personal development, we're simultaneously seeking and establishing important social connections that can affect us for the rest of our lives.

2 Whether you're forging a new friendship with a friendly guy in your Theology class, or you're deepening your friendships with teammates, the people you choose to surround yourself with have a powerful impact on you.

3 As a fortune cookie or artistic Instagram post once said, "Your vibe attracts your tribe." But it's more complicated than that, because your "tribe" also affects your "vibe".

4 There are a lot of benefits of having strong, positive friendships, and it's a lot more than just having someone to hold your hair back after you've had too much to drink or having someone to be your wingman.

5 According to the Mayo Clinic, emotional benefits of friendship include: increased sense of belonging and purpose, boosted happiness, reduced stress, improved self-confidence and self-worth, helping cope with trauma and encouragement to make healthy lifestyle choices.

6 Research shows that smaller social networks and greater loneliness can increase your risk for substance abuse, health problems and even mortality.

⁷ But remember: There's a difference between being alone and being lonely.

⁸ Not everyone wants to be surrounded by people all the time. Some of us get energy from being around others, and some of us need alone time to recharge. Whatever you need to be happy and healthy is what you should do. But when being alone turns into feeling lonely—that's when it's important to find your friends.

⁹ And there are benefits of having strong social support, but it doesn't mean you should try to be friends with everyone. Friends can be sources of stress and can be negative influences as well, so it's important to choose our friends wisely.

¹⁰ But how do you find friends?

¹¹ Freshmen Orientation is one of the first places we made friends at UP. Between built-in friendship options like roommates and floor mates and endless awkward ice-breakers, there are a lot of opportunities to make friends in our freshman year.

¹² By sophomore year, you've established a couple of close friends and an array of other social connections: peripheral friends, acquaintances, lab partners, coworkers, teammates and crushes.

¹³ During junior year, you've deepened your friendships. You're probably closer to some of your friends than you've been with others in the past. You may have had to help a friend deal with a messy breakup, or they may have helped you overcome the loss of a loved one.

¹⁴ By senior year, you have your friends. They know you better than anyone, and you trust them with your biggest fears and insecurities. When you go to class, you recognize most of the people in the room.

¹⁵ But sometimes, life doesn't work out smoothly. Friendships don't get to develop. Your best friend transfers. Your lab partner drops the class. Friends

become distant acquaintances. Girlfriends become ex-girlfriends. Your crush graduates early before you can confess your love for them.

16 Sometimes you have to make new friends. Sometimes it's easy. But sometimes there's not a bubbly blonde girl at the party asking to play a card game and be best friends forever. Sometimes you have to push yourself outside your comfort zone in order to create new friendships. Chances are meeting new people won't be as scary as you think it will be. If you're genuine and kind, most people will want to be your friend anyway.

17 Here are some ideas of how to make friends in non-awkward ways:

1) Attend an event on campus. Lecturers hold discussions in Buckley Center practically every month. And if nothing else, CPB movies and Pilots After Dark are weekly staples in campus life.

2) Volunteer. The Moreau Center has so many opportunities for students to volunteer their time in the community. If you go through the Moreau Center, they'll probably connect you with other students, and if someone's volunteering, they're probably a good person and would make a great friend.

3) Join a club. UP has a club for everything: comic books, gardening, treasure hunting ... You name it.

4) Accept invitations. How many times have you received a Facebook invitation to a party or discussion group or movie screening? Instead of ignoring that little red notification, click on it, say you're "Going" and then go! And if that's not your style.

5) Create the invitation yourself. Sometimes people don't know we want to hang out until we ask them. Ask a classmate if they want to get coffee after class or if that guy in your dorm wants to get breakfast sometime.

18 Ultimately, the effort it takes to make new friends is worth it. Your mind and body depend on your social supports. You can't do this alone—and you don't have to.

Source: We all need friends [Editorial]. (2016, January). *The Beacon*. Retrieved January 10, 2020, from https://www.toriupbeacon.com/article/2016/01/editorial.

Language and Culture

The **University of Portland** (**UP**) is a private Catholic university in Portland, Oregon. It was founded in 1901 and enrolls approximately 4,200 students. The campus  is located in the University Park neighborhood near St. Johns, on a bluff overlooking the Willamette River. With a college of arts and sciences, a graduate school, and schools of business, education, engineering and nursing, it is the only comprehensive Catholic university in Oregon.

Language and Culture

Campus Program Board (**CPB**) is a student-run organization that plans unique events for University of Portland students. From concerts to  dances, and it brings the fun with the goal of providing unforgettable experiences.

Pilots After Dark

During the school year, **Pilots After Dark** provides UP students with late night programming every Friday and Saturday night from 10 p.m. -1 a.m. in the Pilot House. Students can expect local bands, trivia, karaoke, comedy, and more.

Moreau Center Moreau Center for Service and Justice

In partnership with local and global communities, the Moreau Center for Service and Justice engages critical human and environmental concerns through active learning, mutually beneficial service, and experience-based leadership development rooted in Catholic social teaching.

Find more on website: https://www.up.edu/

News - Moreau Center

Moreau Center for Service & Justice honored as one of the "Top Schools for Service" by Catholic Volunteer Network

`Moreau Center` `Awards and Rankings`

April 23, 2020

University of Portland's Moreau Center for Service & Justice was honored by the Catholic Volunteer Network as one of their "Top Schools for Service". In honor of National Volunteer Week, the Catholic Volunteer Network put together a list of schools who "demonstrated consistent excellence in collaborating with our network and championing post-grad service among students."

Task A | Reading Comprehension Strategy: Skimming for gist

What is skimming?

◇ **Skimming** is glancing as quickly as possible over a text looking for what the text is generally about. In real life, when we pick up a book, we might skim through it to decide whether it's what we want. We might skim a row of brochures to see if there are any about a subject we're interested in. When we pick up a newspaper, we might also skim over the front page to see if there's anything worth reading. To skim efficiently, you should pay attention to headings in the text, the first and last sentence of each paragraph, you may need to sweep your eyes over pages using your forefinger to rapidly move over the page in a zig-zag pattern.

Exercise

Skim through the passage and put the following notes a – h taken from the passage in the order in which they appear in the passage.

- ( ) a. not frightening to meet new people as it is thought to be
- ( ) b. invite classmates for a drink after a class
- ( ) c. you and people around you affect each other
- ( ) d. being alone makes some people energetic
- ( ) e. periodic events offer a good chance for a friendship
- ( ) f. friendship facilitates tackling of difficult situation
- ( ) g. friendship fails to deepen sometimes
- ( ) h. first-year students make friends during orientation

Task B | Language Spotlight: Citations and quotations

In academic writing, materials from other sources are used to support viewpoints. The use of a source is known as a citation. To avoid plagiarism, a reference should be included to make clear where the material is from.

Exercises

1. Match the following two sentences taken from the passage with two forms of citation: direct quotation which uses exactly the same words as the source, and paraphrase which uses the author's own language.

    ( ) As a fortune cookie or artistic Instagram post once said, "Your vibe attracts your tribe."
    ( ) According to the Mayo Clinic, emotional benefits of friendships include: increased sense of belonging and purpose, boosted happiness, reduced stress, improved self-confidence and self-worth, help coping with trauma and encouragement to make healthy lifestyle choices.

    When referring to sources, more than one style of citation can be used.
    1) statement + reference
    e. g. Marx believed that "capitalism is very unequal" (Wetherly and Otter 2011, p. 341).
    2) author-focus
    e. g. As reported by/According to Wetherly and Otter (2011, p. 341), Marx believed that capitalism is very unequal.

2. Decide which style of citation is used in the following sentence and rewrite it in an alternative style.

    "One view is that in countries, people's incomes have risen steadily." (Bowles, Edwards, and Roosevelt, 2005, p. 8)"

You may rewrite like this: _____

_____

_____

Task C | Vocabulary Practice: Words with hyphens

1. Identify all the hyphenated words from the passage and note them down in the following box. Work with your partner in pairs to see if you have noted down the same words.

Notes

2. Complete the following sentences using hyphenated words from the passage.
   1) Some general social talk is a good _____ and bridge-builder in this respect.
   2) Do not ever talk about dates you have had with other people or your _____.
   3) She never went beyond the high school diploma that allowed her to find work as an account, because she lacked _____.
   4) Here are the tips for socializing with your co-workers in a _____ way.
   5) Each design agent includes a neural network to detect novelty, but different agents have different _____ preferences for novelty.

3. Complete the following sentences using given hyphenated words.

up-to-date   back-to-back   head-to-toe   best-kept   little-known

   1) Biographers are good at discovering _____ facts.
   2) A lonely island in the middle of the South Atlantic conceals Charles Darwin's _____ secret.
   3) The most essential element of any job search is an _____ resume.
   4) Canada is holding _____ summits—doubling the cost.
   5) These traditional _____ garments have been vilified in the West as symbols of oppression.

4. Read the following sentences and decide if hyphenation in each of them is correctly used or not, if not, try to correct it.

> ***Hyphens*** are used internally in some compound words to separate the words forming the compound word, such as merry-go-round, editor-in-chief. Hyphens connect the words of a compound modifier that comes before the word being modified. Hyphens are not used this way with compound parts ending in *-ly* or made up of proper nouns or proper adjectives.

1) That man is well-respected. (   )
2) That was a badly-punctuated sentence. (   )
3) The South-American rain forest is home to hundreds of species of hummingbirds. (   )

Task D | Critical Thinking: Commenting on the friendship and love on campus

1. Work in groups, and have a further discussion on the following questions:
   1) What is campus friendship? What is campus love?
   2) What are the differences between campus love and campus friendship?
   3) How do you balance friendship and love on campus?
   4) What will you do if you and your best friend fall in love with the same one on campus?
2. Take notes in the following box and make a written report on results of the above discussion.

Notes

Reading 2

Differences Between Love and Friendship

¹ Love is a strong emotion. It is a wide array of feelings directed towards another person or object. It can pertain to personal attraction in the case of people in a romantic relationship and attachment in the case of family and friends. It is the foundation of interpersonal relationships that are built between family, friends, and partners.

² Love may also refer to compassion, which is mainly geared towards the protection and promotion of common good. Love may also be directed towards other beings and ideas such as animals, plants, music, and arts.

³ Friendship, on the other hand, is a relationship involving a variety of feelings. It is a mutual affection that forms an intrapersonal bond between people. Friendship also involves one's ability to establish good camaraderie towards his/her peers through effective communication, mutual understanding, and compassion.

⁴ Additionally, a friendship's foundation includes sympathy, empathy, honesty, altruism, affection, and love. Friendship, unlike romantic relationships, is purely platonic in nature.

⁵ So what's the difference between love and friendship?

⁶ Firstly, love is an emotion or a feeling while friendship is a relationship.

Although love is a strong feeling of attraction towards another person, it does not necessarily mean that two people should be in a relationship when they are in love. On the contrary, individuals cannot call each other friends without establishing a relationship rooted in trust and honesty.

7 Love exists in different forms. Love can be directed towards a family member, a friend, a significant other, a country, or an ideology. Meanwhile, friendship can be the foundation for different kinds of relationships, including relationships with family members, friends, and a significant other.

8 In addition to that, unlike friendship, love typically involves a deeper level of attachment. Any signs of detachment can significantly impact a person who deeply loves his/her significant other.

9 Furthermore, romantic love is exclusive to two people. Friendship, by contrast, may involve two or more people. Also, friendship is purely platonic in nature. Romantic love, by contrast, may involve a sexual or physical relationship.

10 Love can be felt towards everyone without needing to establish any kind of relationship with them. This kind of love is portrayed through compassion. On the other hand, friendship requires a stronger degree of association.

Source: Differences between love and friendship [Editorial]. (2017, November 18). *Difference. Guru.* Retrieved March 1, 2021, from https://difference.guru/difference-between-love-and-friendship/.

Task A | Reading Comprehension Strategy: Summarizing

Summarizing helps readers pay attention to essential ideas and consolidate important supportins details, enables them to focus on key words and phrases that are worth noting and remembering, and gives readers a more concise understanding and a longer memory. It requires readers to identify the most important ideas in a text, ignore information that is irrelevant, and integrate the central ideas in a meaningful way.

Exercise

Read through the passage and summarize it by filling in the blanks of the following summary table.

Love	Friendship
Love is a/an _____ or a feeling.	Friendship is a/an _____ between people.
Love is directed to a/an _____ member, a friend, a significant other, a country, or an ideology.	Friendship can be the best _____ for different kinds of relationships, including relationships with family members, friends, and a significant other.
Love involves a deeper level of _____.	Friendship does _____ involve a deeper level of attachment.
Romantic love is _____ to two people.	Friendship may _____ two or more people.
Romantic love may involve a sexual or _____ relationship.	Friendship is _____ (nonsexual or nonphysical).
Love can be felt towards every one _____ needing to establish any kind of relationship.	Friendship requires a stronger degree of _____.

Task B | Language Spotlight: Language for contrasts

1. Look at the sentence taken from the fourth paragraph of the passage: "Friendship, unlike romantic relationships, is purely platonic in nature." In this sentence, the word "unlike" is used to describe a contrast between friendship and romantic love. Read the whole passage, identify all the language expressions used for contrasting differences and note them down in the following box.

Notes

2. Classify all the expressions you have identified for contrasting differences into different groups of the table, and add to each group with other language expressions you have known.

Preposition	Conjunction	Adverb/Adverbial phrase

3. Complete the following short paragraph by using as many different expressions for contrasting differences as possible.

So what is the difference between love and hate? Love is a positive feeling, _____ hate is a negative one. In its active form, love is creative and protective, _____ in its active form, hate is destructive. Most often, individuals who love tend to show it in an active way. For example, if you love a song, you cannot help but hum along to it or tap your foot. _____, people who hate tend to be more passive about it. For example, you may hate a song, but you leave the radio on because someone else likes it or you may hate that guy from the second floor but you still say "hello" because it's polite.

Task C | Vocabulary Practice: Verbs related to giving definitions

1. Complete the following sentences using the expressions from the passage.
   1) It (love) can _____ to personal attraction in the case of people in a romantic relationship and attachment in the case of family and friends.
   2) Love may also _____ to compassion, which is mainly geared towards the protection and promotion of common good.
   3) Friendship also _____ one's ability to establish good camaraderie towards his/her peers through effective communication, mutual understanding, and compassion.
   4) It (friendship) _____ a mutual affection _____ forms an intrapersonal bond between people.
2. Try to use other language expressions which are commonly used in academic texts for giving definitions to rewrite the above 4 sentences in Activity 1.

e. g. ... is/can be defined as ...

1) _____

2) _____

3) _____

4) _____

3. Work in pairs, take turns to use a different expression to define the following terms with the given information.
   1) motivation/direction and intensity of one's effort
   2) MOOC/course of study made available over the Internet to a very large number of people
   3) Tok-tok/sort of gamified video-sharing social app that hooks younger demographics, at least at first

   1) _____

   2) _____

   3) _____

Task D | Critical Thinking: Contrasting between two forms of love

⟶ It is said that when referring to love between two different people, there are in fact two distinct forms of love: platonic love and romantic love.

Discussion

1. Work in groups, and have a further discussion on the following questions:
   1) What is platonic love? What is romantic love? Try to define them.
   2) What are the differences between platonic love and romantic love?
   3) Do you think two partners who have been in romantic love can continue to be friends after breaking up?

2. Take notes in the following box and make a written report on results of the above discussion.

Notes

Glossary of Unit 3

Reading 1

simultaneously
adv. at the same instant
e. g. The TV show launched simultaneously with an iPhone app of the same name.

forge
v. to create a relationship or new conditions
e. g. The two women forged a close bond.

tribe
n. a group of persons having a common character, occupation, or interest
e. g. The wedding joined the two tribes together.

boost
v. to increase or raise
e. g. That boosted the cost of imports and sped up inflation.

trauma
n. an emotional wound or shock often having long-lasting effects
e. g. She never fully recovered from the traumas she suffered during her childhood.

abuse
n. improper or excessive use
e. g. He subjected his wife to physical and emotional abuse.

mortality
n. the ratio of deaths in an area to the population of that area, expressed per 1,000 per year
e. g. The government is trying to reduce infant mortality.

orientation
n. an act of introducing a new situation or environment
e. g. These materials are for the orientation of new employees.

awkward
adj. not at ease socially; unsure and constrained in manner
e. g. The start of the happy hour can be a little awkward.

sophomore
n. a second-year undergraduate
e. g. Lauren is now a sophomore at DePauw University.

genuine
adj. not pretended; sincerely felt or expressed
e. g. His apology seemed genuine.

ultimately
adv. as the end result of a succession or process
e. g. The changes ultimately proved to be unnecessary.

pertain
v. to have to do with or be relevant to
e.g. These books pertain to the country's history.

mutual
adj. concerning each of two or more persons or things; especially given or done in return
e.g. Mutual love and respect was the key to their successful marriage.

compassion
n. a deep awareness of and sympathy for another's suffering

e.g. My parents raised me in the best environment possible, a house full of love, compassion, and kindness.

platonic
adj. relating to, or being a relationship marked by the absence of romance or sex
e.g. They had a platonic friendship, not a romantic one.

exclusive
adj. not divided or shared with others
e.g. Residents have exclusive use of the beach.

What's the Difference Between Friendship and Love?

The line between friendship and love is difficult to draw.

Defining friendship

Friendship is notoriously difficult to define. For Aristotle, friendship, or *philia*, is a virtue which is "most necessary with a view to living ... for without friends no one would choose to live though he had all other goods." For a person to be friends with another, he says, "it is necessary that [they] bear good will to each other and wish good things for each other, without this escaping their notice."

A person may bear good will to another for one of three reasons: that he is good (that is, rational and virtuous), that he is pleasant, or that he is useful. While Aristotle leaves room for the idea that relationships based on advantage alone or pleasure alone can give rise to friendships, he believes that such relationships have a lesser claim to be called friendships than those that are based partly or wholly on virtue. "Those who wish good things to their friends for the sake of the latter are friends most of all, because they do so because of their friends themselves, not coincidentally."

Friendships that are based partly or wholly on virtue are desirable not only because they are associated with a high degree of mutual benefit, but also because they associated with companionship, dependability, and trust. More important still, to be in such a friendship is to exercise reason and virtue, which is the distinctive function of human beings, and which, in Aristotle's system, amounts to happiness.

In Plato's *Lysis*, Socrates says that he should "greatly prefer a real friend to all the gold of Darius", thereby signifying not only that he places friendship on the same high pedestal as philosophy, to which he has devoted (and will sacrifice) his life, but also that the kind of friendship which he has in mind is so rare and uncommon that even he does not possess it. For Plato, friendship ultimately escapes definition because it is more a process than an object. Real friends seek together to live truer, fuller lives by relating to each other authentically and by teaching each other about the limitations of their beliefs and the defects in their character, which are a far greater source of error than mere rational confusion. For Socrates as for Plato, friendship and philosophy are aspects of one and the same impulse, one and the same love: the love that seeks to know.

Defining love

If friendship is hard to define, love is even more so, not least because there are several types of love. Most present in modern minds is *eros*, which is sexual or passionate love. In Greek myth, eros is a form of madness brought about by one of Cupid's arrows. The arrow breaches us and we "fall" in love, as did Paris with Helen, leading to the Trojan War and the downfall of Troy. In modern times, *eros* has been amalgamated with the broader life force, something akin to Schopenhauer's will, a fundamentally blind process of striving for survival and reproduction. Eros has also been contrasted with Logos, or Reason, with Cupid depicted as a blindfolded child.

Until perhaps the 19th century, people thought of love more in terms of *agape* than *eros*.

Agape is universal love, such as the love for strangers, nature, or God. Also called charity by Christian thinkers, it can be said to encompass the modern concept of altruism, defined as unselfish concern for the welfare of others. *Agape* helps to build and maintain the psychological, social, and, indeed, environmental fabric that shields, sustains, and enriches us. Given the increasing anger and division in our society, and the state of our planet, we could all do with more old-fashioned *agape*.

There are also other types of love, most notably *storge* and *pragma*. *Storge*, or familial love, is the love between parents and their children. More broadly, it is the fondness born out of familiarity or dependency and, unlike *philia* or *eros*, does not depend on our personal qualities. People in the early stages of a romantic relationship often expect unconditional storge, but find only the objectifying *eros*, and, if they are lucky, a certain degree of *philia*. Over time, *eros* often mutates into *storge* and, if we are lucky, there is some *philia* as well.

Pragma is a kind of practical love founded on reason or duty and one's longer-term interests. Sexual attraction takes a back seat in favor of personal qualities and compatibilities, shared goals, and making it work. In the days of arranged marriages, *pragma* must have been very common. Although unfashionable, it remains widespread, most visibly in certain high-profile celebrity and political pairings.

In conclusion

So where is the boundary between friendship and love? Actually, I think that the higher kind of *philia* that is based partly or wholly on virtue has a much stronger claim to the name of love than *eros*, not least because *eros* is much more selfish and objectifying.

Friendship is not different from love, but the best kind of love.

Source: Schrader, J. (2017, March). What are the differences between love and friendship. *Psychology Today*. Retrieved March 22, 2021, from https://www.psychologytoday.com/us/blog/hide-and-seek/201703.

Unit 4

Choice on Lifestyles

The term "lifestyle" defines how we live. It refers to how we make our homes, how we relate to the world around us, and how we raise our children, manage our health and make a living. In this unit, you will examine issues that may influence the lifestyle choices. You will learn that a lifestyle choice is not only a personal decision but also involves a number of factors. You will look at features that are typical in an academic context, such as, linking words, referencing, reporting verbs, essay patterns, etc. and will practice using them appropriately.

By the end of this unit, you will be able to:

SKILL	TASK
practice skimming skills to get general ideas	• Reading 1 • Task A
identify the sentence that introduces the main idea of the article	• Reading 1 • Task A
learn to use appropriate prepositions and language to describe statistics	• Reading 1 • Task B
use appropriate collocations to describe trends or changes	• Reading 1 • Task B
identify and evaluate cohesive devices in a text	• Reading 1 • Task C
learn to examine the reality and the choice of your future lifestyle	• Reading 1 • Task D
identify an SPSE pattern of a text	• Reading 2 • Task A
establish two types of structure for an SPSE essay—block and chain	• Reading 2 • Task A
learn to recognize and review the two elements of references	• Reading 2 • Task B
understand the meaning of a range of reporting verbs for referencing and use them appropriately	• Reading 2 • Task B
learn to reflect on other text patterns, e.g. a cause-effect pattern	• Reading 2 • Tasks C, D

Reading 1

Life Has Become Harder for Young Families

¹ Young people today are delaying starting "adult" life until later and later. The median age of first marriage has climbed to nearly 30, up from the mid-20s a generation ago. The median age of the first-time homebuyer hit a record 33 in 2019, while the average age for women having a baby climbed to 26.9 in 2018, up from 22.7 in 1980. Clearly there are plenty of cultural changes that influence such shifts, but we shouldn't underestimate the added burdens created by government overreach that make it more difficult for young people to settle down and start a family.

College Debt

² In higher education, as with healthcare, a system increasingly reliant on third-party payers for the expenses has been a major driver of <u>exploding</u> tuition costs. In 2018–2019, according to College Board, undergraduate and graduate students received a total of $246 billion in student aid in the form of grants, tax credits and loans.

³ Indeed, there's been a <u>stunning</u> 416 percent rise in total federal, state and institutional student aid loans since 1989, adjusted for inflation. Pell Grants, the federal government's largest college grant tuition assistance program nearly tripled in real terms during that time.

⁴ With billions in federal student aid, grants and below-market interest loans courtesy of the US Department of Education artificially inflating demand for college, tuition prices were sure to explode.

⁵ From 1993 to 2018, consumer expenditures on higher education exploded by 260 percent, roughly 4.5 times as fast as overall consumer expenditures[1].

⁶ One obvious result is higher student loan debt. In an article published by Salon, former Labor Secretary Robert Reich notes, "the average graduate carries a <u>whopping</u> $28,000 in student loan debt", and that as a generation, "millennials are more than one trillion dollars in the red".

⁷ Making matters worse is that a <u>significant</u> share of recent graduates are not earning enough to afford the debt payments. Young people are often drawn into college on the promise that a college degree is their only ticket to career success. But increasingly, it is not. As Ohio University economist Richard Vedder has written, "The Federal Reserve Bank of New York said that 41.4 percent of recent college graduates in December 2018 were 'underemployed', doing jobs mostly held by those with lesser education." In other words, more than two-fifths of recent graduates are in jobs that don't require a college degree. As Vedder notes, this is because "we actually have too many college graduates for the number of professional, managerial, and technical jobs available".

⁸ With a glut of college graduates flooding the job market, there is little bargaining power for millennials entering the job market, outside of those with degrees in highly technical areas. In too many cases, a college degree simply does not translate into earning power sufficient enough to pay off <u>formidable</u> student loans. And that glut can in no small part be attributed to the massive sums of money flowing from government programs.

Housing

⁹ With many young folks already strapped with <u>large</u> college loan debts and starting salaries ill equipped to pay it back, taking on a mortgage is something many are increasingly reluctant to do.

¹⁰ And taking that next step is made even more difficult by rapidly <u>rising</u> housing prices. Housing expenditures climbed by 95 percent from 1993 to 2018, far outpacing overall consumer expenditures[2].

¹¹ Overly zealous housing regulations have restricted supply, especially in growing urban areas where new professionals tend to migrate. The increasingly strict local government regulations have driven up the cost of building new homes in many large metro areas.

¹² Young potential homebuyers are priced out of the housing market by spiraling prices, despite the low interest rates. Moreover, many are reluctant to add a mortgage to their already imposing student loan debt.

Day Care

¹³ As if struggling with student loans and escalating housing costs wasn't enough, young people are then confronted with the high costs of raising children. Specifically, costs of day care have been soaring, thanks in large part to government intervention in that market.

¹⁴ According to a 2019 *Atlantic* article, "per-child spending on childcare increased by a factor of 21 from the 1970s to the 2000s". And more recently, "The Census Bureau has found that child-care expenditures rose more than 40 percent from 1990 to 2011, during a period when middle-class wages stagnated. Since the 1990s, childcare costs have grown twice as fast as overall inflation."

¹⁵ The *Atlantic* article attributes a part of child care's hefty price tag to the industry being "highly regulated", further noting that "states with strict labor laws tend to have the most expensive facilities".

¹⁶ Caregiver-to-child ratio requirements are probably the most expensive regulatory mandate. But state licensed child care centers are burdened with massive amounts of intricate, complex, and often puzzling regulations, some of which even list as many as nearly 200 pages of "child care rules". Such requirements limit the supply of day cares. The more personnel required per child (and thus per facility) means the available workers must be consolidated into fewer facilities.

¹⁷ Meanwhile, rapidly growing government subsidies serve to inflate the

demand for childcare. Head Start, the federal government's cornerstone free day care program for low-income children, spent nearly $9.9 billion in 2018.

[18] Naturally, with so much government funding being directed into the day care industry, demand is propped up significantly. States also add subsidies and free day care programs of their own.

[19] The significant government interventions restricting supply and inflating demand will naturally serve to drive prices upward. Middle class families are squeezed the most, as they are taxed to pay for the subsidies and free programs but earn too much to receive the benefits—and then are forced to pay the inflated prices to boot.

Conclusion

[20] The trends are clear: young people today are starting "adult life" and families at a later age. The debate of whether this is good or bad for society is beyond the scope of this article. But like many other broad cultural shifts, this can in no small part be attributed to the influence of a leviathan government too.

Source: Thomas, B. (2020, March 28). How governments make life harder for young families. *Mises Wire*. Retrieved April 5, 2020, from https://mises.org/wire.

Task A | Reading Comprehension Strategy: Skimming for gist

1. The lifestyle is the living conditions, behaviour, and habits that are typically chosen by a particular person or a group of people. Work in pairs. Describe your dream lifestyle to your partner and make notes about it below.

My dream lifestyle	My partner's dream lifestyle
1.	1.
2.	2.
3.	3.
4.	4.
5.	5.

2. Work with your partner. Discuss some possible factors or obstacles that may make it difficult for you and your partner to choose a dream lifestyle in the future. Take notes below.

Factors that may influence the choice of a dream lifestyle
1.
2.
3.
4.
5.

3. Skim through the passage. Work with a partner and answer the following questions.
   1) In which country do the young people mentioned in the article live?
   2) Identify the sentence that introduces the main idea of the article.
   3) What contributes to the fact that young people are starting a family at a later age?
4. List the different ages when young people start a family.
   The average age of first marriage now: _____ vs _____ a generation ago
   The average age of the first-time buying a house in 2019: _____
   The average age for women having a baby in 2018: _____ vs _____ in 1980

English Reading for Academic Purposes 1A

Task B | Language Spotlight: Describing trends and statistics

1. Work with your partner. Study the usage of the prepositions in the following graphs.

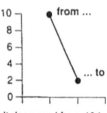

It decreased from 10 to 2.

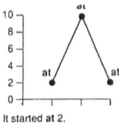

It started at 2.
It peaked at 10.
It finished at 2.

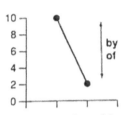

There was a drop of 8.
It dropped by 8.

2. Complete the sentences using appropriate prepositions. Compare your work with a partner.
   1) During the summer, student numbers at the school fluctuate _____ 150 and 170 per week.
   2) The last decade has seen a steep increase _____ the number of people diagnosed with diabetes.
   3) The unemployment rate in this country dropped _____ 30% due to the coronavirus pandemic.
   4) The number of car sales hit the lowest point _____ 50 last month.
   5) There has been a dramatic decline _____ 30% in the retail business during the crisis.

3. Identify appropriate adjectives or participles from the article to fill in the blanks.
   1) a major driver of _____ tuition costs
   2) a _____ 416 percent rise in total federal, state and institutional student aid loans
   3) a _____ $28,000 in student loan debt
   4) a _____ share of recent graduates
   5) to pay off _____ student loans
   6) (to be) strapped with _____ college loan debts
   7) rapidly _____ housing prices
   8) in _____ urban areas
   9) (to be) priced out of the housing market by _____ prices
   10) struggling with student loans and _____ housing costs
   11) (to be) confronted with the _____ costs of raising children
   12) (to) attribute a part of child care's _____ price tag to the industry being "highly regulated"
   13) (to be) burdened with _____ amounts of intricate, complex, and often

puzzling regulations
14) rapidly _____ government subsidies
15) with so _____ government funding being directed into the day care industry

Task C | Vocabulary Practice: Cohesive devices

Study the following explanations, definitions and synonyms of the linking words from the article and match them with the linking words in the box.

> **What are cohesive devices?**
>
> ➢ *Cohesive devices*, sometimes called linking words, linkers, connectors, discourse markers or transitional words, are used to link ideas grammatically and lexically within a text or a sentence and hold a text together.

| clearly | indeed | in other words | moreover |
| specifically | meanwhile | naturally |

1) Used to emphasize a statement or response confirming something already suggested:
   _____
   Synonyms: certainly, undoubtedly, undeniably

2) Used to add more detailed or exact information: _____
   Synonyms: particularly, in particular, especially

3) Putting it differently, usually more simply or explicitly: _____
   Synonyms: namely, i.e., put it differently

4) In addition to what has been said: _____
   Synonyms: furthermore, besides, in addition

5) As may be expected, of course: _____
   Synonyms: as anticipated, as expected, spontaneously

6) Without equivocation; decidedly: _____
   Synonyms: obviously, evidently, certainly, without doubt, undoubtedly, undeniably

7) While something else is happening: _____

Synonyms: in the meantime, for the moment, concurrently, at the same time

---

Task D | Critical Thinking: Evaluating the content of a text

Discussion

Work in groups and discuss the questions. Give reasons to support your views.

1. Do you think the information in the article is reliable? Why do you say so?
2. What else will influence young generation's choice of lifestyle in addition to the financial burden demonstrated in the article?

My main points	My partner's main points
1.	1.
2.	2.
3.	3.
4.	4.
5. …	5. …

Reading 2

Obesity and Poor Fitness

¹ Consumption of processed and convenience foods and our dependence on the car have led to an increase in obesity and reduction in the fitness level of the adult population. In some countries, especially industrialized ones, the number of obese people can amount to one third of the population (WHO, 2015). This is significant as obesity and poor fitness lead to a decrease in life expectancy, and it is therefore important for individuals and governments to work together to tackle this issue and improve their citizens' diet and fitness.

² Obesity and poor fitness decrease life expectancy. Overweight people are more likely to have serious illnesses such as diabetes and heart disease, which can result in premature death (Wilson, 2014). It is well known that regular exercise can reduce the risk of heart disease and stroke, which means that those with poor fitness levels are at an increased risk of suffering from those problems.

³ Changes by individuals to their diet and their physical activity can increase life expectancy. There is a reliance today on the consumption of processed foods, which have a high fat and sugar content. According to Peterson (2013), preparing their own foods, and consuming more fruit and vegetables, people could ensure that their diets are healthier and more balanced, which could lead to a reduction in obesity levels. In order to improve fitness levels, people could choose to walk or cycle to work or to the shops rather than taking the car. They could also choose to walk upstairs instead of taking the lift. These simple changes could lead to a significant improvement in fitness levels.

⁴ Governments could also implement initiatives to improve their citizens' eating and exercise habits. Jones (2011) argues that this could be done through education, for example by adding classes to the curriculum about healthy diet and lifestyles. Governments could also do more to encourage their citizens to walk or cycle instead of taking the car, for instance by building more cycle lanes or increasing vehicle taxes. In short, obesity and poor fitness are a significant problem in modern life, leading to lower life expectancy. Individuals and governments can work together to tackle this problem and so improve diet and fitness. Of the solutions suggested, those made by individuals themselves are likely to have more impact, though it is clear that a concerted effort with the government is essential for success. With obesity levels in industrialized and industrializing countries continuing to rise, it is essential that we take action now to deal with this problem.

References

Jones, J. (2011). Educate for obesity. *The Educationalist Journal.* 8(4). pp34–56.

Peterson, R.J. (2013). Healthier eating creates a healthier world. *The New Scientist.* 76(6).

Wilson, C. (2014). Diseases connected to obesity. *Medical Journal.* 55(5). pp23–56.

World Health Organisation (WHO). (2015). Obesity the epidemic. [online] Available at: http://www.WHO.uk/obesityguidelines [Accessed 10 October 2015].

Source: Obesity. (n.d.). *AEUK*. Retrieved April 20, 2020, from https://academic-englishuk.com/.

Task A | Reading Comprehension Strategy: Pattern of the essay

Work with a partner, complete the blanks and identify the pattern of this essay.

Situation:
_____ + _____
⬇
_____ + _____
⬇
_____

Problem:

_____ → _____

_____ → _____

Solution:
By individuals:
1. _____.
2. _____.

By government:
1. _____.
2. _____.

Conclusion:
_____

Evaluation:
_____

English Reading for Academic Purposes 1A

Pattern of an essay

➢ Finding the patterns helps you follow the main idea. Thus, looking for patterns is an effective way to improve your comprehension while reading. From this unit and beyond, you will learn to recognize some basic patterns that are used in developing ideas.

➢ Reading 2 is an essay organized by an SPSE (Situation Problem Solution Evaluation) pattern. Problem solving is all about using logic, as well as imagination, to make sense of a situation and come up with an intelligent solution. The aim of the SPSE essay is to examine a problem and discuss two or more possible solutions. You will end with a judgement evaluating the effectiveness of these solutions.

➢ There are two main ways to structure an SPSE essay: a block or a chain structure.

➢ For the block structure, all of the problems are listed first, and all of the solutions are listed afterwards.

➢ For the chain structure, each problem is followed immediately by the solution to that problem.

➢ Both types of structure have their merits. The former is generally clearer, especially for shorter essays, as you may have found out from Reading 2, while the latter ensures that any solutions you present relate directly to the problems you have given.

⮕ The two types of structure, block and chain, are shown in the diagrams below.

A Block Structure

- Introduction (including "situation")
- Problem 1
- Problem 2
- ……
- Transition sentence/paragraph
- Solution 1
- Solution 2
- ……
- Conclusion (including "evaluation")

A Chain Structure

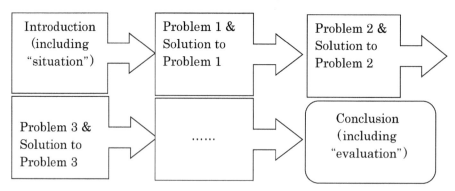

Task B | Language Spotlight: Review of referencing within an article

1. As you have learned in Unit 2, referencing is a consistent method of acknowledging another person's ideas which you have used in your own writing. You must reference all sources that you use in your work, including words and ideas, facts, images, videos, audio, websites, statistics, diagrams and data.
   - Compare the references from Reading 2:

Citation within the article

1. In some countries, especially industrialized ones, the number of obese people can amount to one third of the population (WHO, 2015).
2. Overweight people are more likely to have serious illnesses such as diabetes and heart disease, which can result in premature death (Wilson, 2014).
3. According to Peterson (2013), preparing their own foods, and consuming more fruit and vegetables, people could ensure that their diets are healthier and more balanced, which could lead to a reduction in obesity levels.
4. Jones (2011) argues that this could be done through education, for example, by adding classes to the curriculum about healthy diet and lifestyles.

References at the end of the article
1. Jones, J. (2011). Educate for obesity. *The Educationalist Journal*. 8 (4). pp34 –56.
2. Peterson, R. J. (2013). Healthier eating creates a healthier world. *The New Scientist*. 76 (6).
3. Wilson, C. (2014). Diseases connected to obesity. *Medical Journal*. 55 (5). pp23 –56.
4. World Health Organisation (WHO). (2015). Obesity the epidemic. [online] Available at: http://www. WHO. uk/obesityguidelines [Accessed 10 October 2015].

- As you may find from the boxes above, referencing includes two elements:
  a) A citation within the text indicating that a particular concept phrase or idea has been sourced elsewhere.
  b) A complete reference list giving the full citation details for all sources referred to in the document.
2. Go back to Reading 1, and identify all the sources within the article and at the end of the article.

Task C | Vocabulary Practice: Reporting verbs

1. When incorporating sources into your work, it is important that you use an appropriate reporting verb or structure. Study the following statements, and choose a suitable underlined verb for each explanation.

Exercise

1) As Lynne Davis states (2004), "Stories cement together generations of collective memory, embodying the historical, spiritual, social, and spatial."
2) Henderson (2016) emphasizes that the ability to engage with the thoughts of others is one of the most important skills for writers.
3) Wilson (2019) argues that the same principle ought to apply to research.
4) Hill-Collins (2001) notes that if dominant power operates via intersecting oppressions, resistance must show comparable complexity.
5) McCroskey (2012) and Ali (2017) claim that lack of confidence is the most common barrier to communication.
6) Swain (1998) and Wenger (2002) reject the new theory because it fails to include

important factors from the sociocultural perspective.
7) Clark (2016) questions the effectiveness of developing EFL students' writing skills.
8) Kovach (2007) concludes with a reflection on the implications arising from the inter-relationship between method, ethics, and care when using the conversational method.

[a] to suggest it is inaccurate: _____
[b] to disagree with somebody or a theory: _____
[c] to give reasons for the view: _____
[d] to say directly: _____
[e] to come to the final point or summary: _____
[f] to say just briefly: _____
[g] to say something is true directly, and firmly, often used when others disagree: _____
[h] to highlight an important point: _____

Task D | Critical Thinking: Reflecting on reading patterns

Discussion

Think about the following questions and discuss with your partner.

1. Work in groups, and look again at the pattern of SPSE. Discuss what a cause-effect pattern looks like. Are there also two types? Try to draw a diagram to show how a cause-effect essay is organized.
   Make a note of your discussion below:

2. Work with your partner, and discuss what other preventive measures people can take to live a quality life besides the suggestions offered in Reading 2. You may use a diagram to indicate the interrelationship between the measures and a healthy lifestyle.

Possible preventive measures
1.
2.
3.
4.
5.

Glossary of Unit 4

Reading 1

stunning
adj. extremely surprising or shocking
e. g. Researchers have made a stunning discovery.

whopping
adj. very large, massive, enormous
e. g. Sales rocketed a whopping 845% on March 11 and 12 as states announced lockdowns.

formidable
adj. inspiring fear or respect through being impressively large, powerful, intense, or capable
e. g. The mountains were a formidable barrier.

stagnate
v. to stop developing or making progress
e. g. Most notably, for the last 50 years, their wages have stagnated.

intricate
adj. having a lot of different parts or small details that fit together
e. g. Tsunami generation involves intricate interactions among earthquakes, landslides, and "sympathetic" vibrations between the quake and the ocean above it.

consolidate
v. to join things together into one or to be joined into one
e. g. The two funds will consolidate into one.

leviathan
n. a very large and powerful thing
e. g. The factory is a towering leviathan in the middle of the town.

Reading 2

obesity
n. more than average fatness
e. g. Even for healthy people, keeping your blood sugar in a healthy range can help reduce the risk of obesity and the risk of developing diabetes.

diabetes
n. a medical condition in which someone has too much sugar in their blood
e. g. Trained dogs are capable of detecting other medical conditions including diabetes, Parkinson's disease, malaria and even cancer.

premature
adj. happening before the normal or expected time
e. g. Too much exposure to the sun can cause the premature aging of skin.

implement
v. to make something that has been officially decided start to happen or be used
e. g. States remain years behind in implementing child support regulations.

initiative
n. a new plan for dealing with a particular

problem or for achieving a particular purpose *e. g.* For those who can't afford the help, here are some of the programs, organizations and initiatives that provide small business owners with one-on-one consultations, tools and other support—all free.

Life in Ancient Cities

What was life like in the earliest cities created by humankind? This question has been pondered by archaeologists and historians for centuries. With modern technology, scientific explorers have been able to gain insight into the past. Looking at one of these early civilizations in particular offers an illuminating view of early urban life.

The Indus Valley civilization (circa 3300 – 1700 B. C. E.), also known as the Harappan civilization, was one of the earliest urban civilizations, roughly contemporaneous with those of Mesopotamia, Egypt, and China. It was located in what is now Pakistan and northwest India, on the flood plain of the Indus River.

Although the Harappans had a written language, the Indus script remains undeciphered. Most of what is known about their culture and civilization comes from the ruins of their two largest cities: Harappa and Mohenjo-daro. Both cities cover somewhat less than 2.6 square kilometers (one square mile). Mohenjo-daro has been estimated to have had a population of around 40,000 or more; Harappa was likely around the same.

The Harappan cities did not have palaces or temples, and show no evidence that the society was ruled by hereditary potentates like kings and queens. They may have been governed by elected officials or other elites, such as merchants or landowners.

The cities, located about 644 kilometers (400 miles) from one another, were generally similar in layout. Each city was laid out in a grid-like pattern oriented on a north-south axis. One portion of each city consisted of a citadel mound complex (an area with public buildings raised about 12 meters, or 40 feet, above the floodplain), and a lower town that appears to have been mostly residential.

The citadel mound complex at Mohenjo-daro was oriented on a north-south axis and was about twice as long as it was broad. It appears to have been protected by a wall and fortified with towers made of baked brick. The citadel complex included a structure called the Great Bath, as well as a granary, a residential structure, and assembly buildings.

The Great Bath, which was apparently used for ritual bathing or cleansing, measured around 84 square meters (904 square feet) in area and was about 2.5 meters (8.2 feet) deep. The Great Bath was made watertight through the use of finely cut bricks, gypsum, and bitumen tar.

One of the more significant features of Harappan cities was their sophisticated water supply and waste extraction systems. In Mohenjo-daro, water was supplied from some 700 wells to both public and private facilities.

Most houses in the lower town had their own bathrooms; many had their own wells. The bathrooms were typically arranged against the house's outside wall so both the bath and the toilet could discharge into the municipal sewage network. This municipal sewage network consisted of covered sewers built under the streets with removable covers for access for cleaning. In places where the effluent had to traverse long distances, sump- or cess-pits were provided.

Harappan houses were generally made of brick and varied in size, from single rooms to larger multistory houses with a central courtyard. Some of the larger houses may also have had an open upper deck. Access to the houses was from side streets; the only openings to the main streets were for sewage discharge. Wooden frames were used for doors and windows.

In addition to residences, the lower town housed workshops for artisans, such as dyers, potters, wheelwrights, and the like. In some cases, they were integrated with the residential areas, but in others they were segregated as worker districts.

The primary building materials in Harappan cities were sun-dried and burnt bricks. A standardized brick with a ratio of 4 : 2 : 1 appears to have been common across several cities. Brick was generally laid using alternating rows of bricks laid lengthways and sideways, referred to today as an "English bond".

Staples of the Harappan diet included wheat and barley, as well as rice. The Harappans also grew and ate a variety of vegetables and fruits, including peas, dates, mustard, and sesame. Cattle, domestic fowl, and other animals, including some wild animals, provided meat. The Harappans also ate fish and shellfish, both fresh and dried.

Harappans used clay or terra-cotta pots, plates, cups, bowls, vases, and flasks for food storage and cooking. Some appear to have been handmade, but others were manufactured using a potter's wheel. In addition, the Harappans had plates made from copper and bronze. Artifacts made from gold, bronze, tin, lead, and other metals suggest that the Harappans were skilled metallurgists.

In this regard, one of the most significant finds from Mohenjo-daro is a 10-centimeter (four-inch) tall bronze sculpture of a dancing girl. The "Indus Dancing Girl" depicts a girl wearing arm jewelry, right hand on her hip, and left leg thrust forward. It is considered significant not only because it demonstrates that Harappan metal-workers were familiar with metal blending and casting techniques, but also because it shows that the culture was sufficiently advanced that dance was well-developed as art or entertainment. Other forms of entertainment were a variety of games and toys, including oxcarts with moveable parts, board games, and six-sided dice.

Among the more common artifacts from the Harappan cities were seals made from steatite, a form of talc. The seals typically had images of animals or other decorations. The seals would have been made on a clay tag or pottery and used by merchants to authenticate, or identify, a package. One famous seal depicts Pashupati, which may have been an early representation of the Hindu god Shiva. It shows Pashupati with a horned headdress and a crescent moon on his forehead; the figure is in a yoga-like position.

Some Indus Valley seals have been found in Mesopotamia, evidence that trade with remote areas was an important aspect of the Harappan economy. In addition to Mesopotamia, the Indus Valley civilization was part of a trading network that included Afghanistan, Iran, and Oman. Perhaps because of these trading networks, the Harappans were among the first to develop a system of standardized weights and measurements. The weights were in the shape of small cubes or hexahedrons. The smallest was about 0.87 grams (0.03 ounces) and the most common was about 13.7 grams (0.48 ounces). It is possible they were used in trade and for determining taxes.

Investigations into the Harappan civilization are ongoing. Since 1986 excavations in the Indus Valley under the auspices of the Harappan Archaeological Research Project have made many important discoveries. Artifacts may be found on display at the National Museum in New Delhi, India, as well as museums throughout the world, including the Metropolitan Museum of Art in New York City, United States.

Source: Wilkinson, F. (2020, February 12). Life in ancient cities. *National Geographic*. Retrieved September 12, 2020, from https://www.nationalgeographic.org/article/life-ancient-cities/.

Uncovered History

Whoever controls the past controls the future. Historical myths, legends and folklore are intricately linked with the past of human nature. As a college student, it is important to develop critical thinking skills on controversial historical issues.

In this unit, students are not only required to develop some key important reading skills and identify cause-effect essay patterns but also to think critically on the development of theater and explore the uncovered causes of Titanic Tragedy.

By the end of this unit, you will be able to:	
SKILL	TASK
do speed reading by identifying essay patterns	• Reading 1 • Task A
identify transitional words for causal analysis	• Reading 1 • Task B
use appropriate language to describe theater	• Reading 1 • Task C
learn skills of summarizing and reviewing	• Reading 1 • Task D
do speed reading by scanning	• Reading 2 • Task A
complete a summary	• Reading 2 • Task B
use appropriate language to describe a cruise	• Reading 2 • Task C
make a summary and a comparison	• Reading 2 • Task D

English Reading for Academic Purposes   1A

READING & CRITICAL THINKING

Reading 1

Pre-reading activity

1. Work with your partner and list possible reasons for the development of theater.

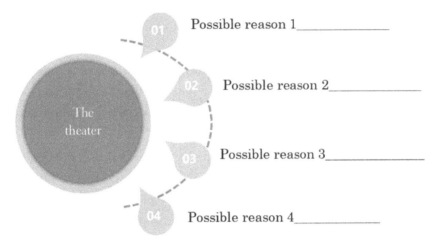

Possible reason 1 _____

Possible reason 2 _____

Possible reason 3 _____

Possible reason 4 _____

2. Read the following text and check your answers against the text.

Note

Unit 5   Uncovered History | 113

The Origins of Theater

¹ In seeking to describe the origins of theater, one must rely primarily on speculation, since there is little concrete evidence on which to draw. The most widely accepted theory, championed by anthropologists in the late nineteenth and early twentieth centuries, envisions theater as emerging out of myth and ritual. The process perceived by these anthropologists may be summarized briefly. During the early stages of its development, a society becomes aware of forces that appear to influence or control its food supply and well-being. Having little understanding of natural causes, it attributes both desirable and undesirable occurrences to supernatural or magical forces, and it searches for means to win the favor of these forces. Perceiving an apparent connection between certain actions performed by the group and the result it desires, the group repeats, refines and formalizes those actions into fixed ceremonies, or rituals.

² Stories (myths) may then grow up around a ritual. Frequently the myths include representatives of those supernatural forces that the rites celebrate or hope to influence. Performers may wear costumes and masks to represent the mythical characters or supernatural forces in the rituals or in accompanying celebrations. As a person becomes more sophisticated, its conceptions of supernatural forces and causal relationships may change. As a result, it may abandon or modify some rites. But the myths that have grown up around the rites may continue as part of the group's oral tradition and may even come to be acted out under conditions divorced from these rites. When this occurs, the first step has been taken toward theater as an autonomous activity, and thereafter entertainment and aesthetic values may gradually replace the former mystical and socially efficacious concerns.

³ Although origin in ritual has long been the most popular, it is by no means the only theory about how the theater came into being. Storytelling has been proposed as one alternative. Under this theory, relating and listening to stories are seen as fundamental human pleasures. Thus, the recalling of an event (a hunt, battle, or other feat) is elaborated through the narrator's pantomime and impersonation and eventually through each role being assumed by a different person.

⁴ A closely related theory sees theater as evolving out of dances that are primarily pantomimic, rhythmical or gymnastic, or from imitations of animal noises and sounds. Admiration for the performer's skill, virtuosity, and grace are seen as motivation for elaborating the activities into fully realized theatrical performances.

⁵ In addition to exploring the possible antecedents of theater, scholars have also theorized about the motives that led people to develop theater. Why did theater develop, and why was it valued after it ceased to fulfill the function of ritual? Most answers fall back on the theories about the human mind and basic human needs. One, set forth by Aristotle in the fourth century BC, sees humans as naturally imitative as taking pleasure in imitating persons, things, and actions and in seeing such imitations. Another, advanced in the twentieth century, suggests that humans have a gift for fantasy, through which they seek to reshape reality into more satisfying forms than those encountered in daily life. Thus, fantasy or fiction (of which drama is one form) permits people to objectify their anxieties and fears, confront them, and fulfill their hopes in fiction if not fact. The theater, then, is one tool whereby people define and understand their world or escape from unpleasant realities.

⁶ But neither the human imitative instinct nor a penchant for fantasy by itself leads to an autonomous theater. Therefore, additional explanations are needed. One necessary condition seems to be a somewhat detached view of human problems. For example, one sign of this condition is the appearance of the comic vision, since comedy requires sufficient detachment to view some deviations from social norms as ridiculous rather than as serious threats to the welfare of the entire group. Another condition that contributes to the development of autonomous theater is the emergence of the aesthetic sense. For example, some early societies ceased to consider certain rites essential to their well-being and abandoned them, nevertheless, they retained as parts of their oral tradition the myths that had grown up around the rites and admired them for their artistic qualities rather than for their religious usefulness.

Source: Johnson, S. Juces. (2018, June). The origins of *The Architect*, pp 30 – 32.

Task A | Reading Comprehension Strategy: Identifying essay patterns

> Identifying essay patterns is an effective skill to do speed reading. This essay is a cause-effect essay, which is a common piece of expository writing showing or explaining the cause and/or effect of something. When we write a cause-effect paper, we are actually making a causal analysis.

Three patterns generally used to organize the body of a cause-effect essay

① multiple causes→single effect pattern
> When we analyze the causes of something, sometimes it may involve a number of factors or multiple causes which produce the single effect. The causes may be unrelated to each other, but all are linked to the effect.
> This pattern starts with an effect and explains its causes. It can be diagramed as follows:

② single cause→multiple effects pattern
> When we do a cause and effect analysis, a cause may produce multiple results or effects which can be illustrated by the following diagram:

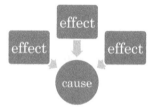

③ the causal chain pattern
> Unlike the multiple cause-and-effect analysis, the causes and effects in a causal chain are always directly related or linked.
> In this pattern, each cause has an effect, which can be the cause of another effect, so on and so forth. This can be illustrated as follows:

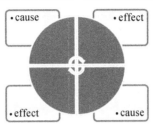

Exercise

Work with a partner, complete the blanks and identify the pattern of this essay.

Situation: _____

Cause 1 _____

Cause 2 _____

Cause 3 _____

Effect _____

Conclusion _____

Task B | Language Spotlight: Transitional expressions for causal analysis

Study the following explanations, definitions and synonyms of the linking words from the article and match them with the linking words in the box.

as a result   attribute   lead to contribute to   since   thereafter
Transitional phrases of preposition: _____ because of, due to, on account of, owing to, as a result of, in consequence of
Transitional phrases of verb: _____ contribute to, lead to, result from, result in, be caused by
Transitional adverbs or adverbial phrases: _____ accordingly, consequently, therefore, thus, thereby, as a result, for this reason
Transitional conjunctions: _____ so, for, since, as, because
Transitional patterns: _____ This is why ..., The reason for ... is that ...

Task C | Vocabulary Practice: Words related to theater

Match the following words related to the theater with definitions.

aesthetic   pantomime   impersonation   rhythmical   gymnastic

1. concerning or characterized by an appreciation of beauty or good taste
2. a performance using gestures and body movements without words
3. a representation of a person that is exaggerated for comic effect
4. recurring with measured regularity
5. vigorously active

Task D | Critical Thinking: Summary and review

Discussion

Think about the following questions and discuss with your partner. You may take notes in the table.

1. In this text the writer has reviewed the historical development of the theater. With the advancement of high technology, do you think the theater will develop in a new form?

2. Work in pairs and list the causes of emergence of theater in China.

Notes

English Reading for Academic Purposes 1A

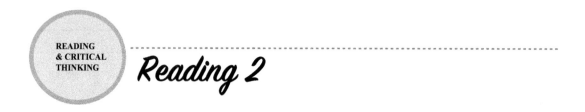

Pre-reading activity

1. Work with your partner, and list the main posible causes for the sinking of the Titanic.

The sinking of the Titanic		
Possible cause 1	Possible cause 2	Possible cause 3

2. Read the following text and check your answers against the text.

Notes

Lessons from the Titanic

¹ From the comfort of our modern lives we tend to look back at the turn of the twentieth century as a dangerous time for sea travelers. With limited communication facilities, and shipping technology still in its infancy in the early nineteen hundreds, we consider ocean travel to have been a risky business. But to the people of the time it was one of the safest forms of transport. At the time of the Titanic's maiden voyage in 1912, there had only been four lives lost in the previous forty years on passenger ships on the North Atlantic crossing. And the Titanic was confidently proclaimed to be unsinkable. She represented the pinnacle of technological advance at the time. Her builders, crew and passengers had no doubt that she was the finest ship ever built. But still she did sink on April 14, 1912, taking 1,517 of her passengers and crew with her.

² The RMS Titanic left Southampton for New York on April 10, 1912. On board were some of the richest and most famous people of the time who had paid large sums of money to sail on the first voyage of the most luxurious ship in the world. Imagine her placed on her end: she was larger at 269 meters than many of the tallest buildings of the day. And with nine decks, she was as high as an eleven storey building. The Titanic carried 329 first class, 285 second class and 710 third class passengers with 899 crew members, under the care of the very experienced Captain Edward J. Smith. She also carried enough food to feed a small town, including 40,000 fresh eggs, 36,000 apples, 111,000 lbs of fresh meat and 2,200 lbs of coffee for the five day journey.

³ RMS Titanic was believed to be unsinkable because the hull was divided into sixteen watertight compartments. Even if two of these compartments flooded, the ship could still float. The ship's owners could not imagine that, in the case of an accident, the Titanic would not be able to float until she was rescued. It was largely as a result of this confidence in the ship and in the safety of ocean travel that the disaster could claim such a great loss of life.

⁴ In the ten hours prior to the Titanic's fatal collision with an iceberg at 11:40 pm, six warnings of icebergs in her path were received by the Titanic's wireless operators. Only one of these messages was formally posted on the bridge; the others were in various locations across the ship. If the combined information in these messages of iceberg positions had been plotted, the ice field which lay across the Titanic's path would have been apparent. Instead, the lack of formal procedures for dealing with information from a relatively new piece of technology, the wireless, meant that the danger was not known until too late. This was not the fault of the Titanic crew. Procedures for dealing with warnings received through the wireless had not been formalized across the shipping industry at the time. The fact that the wireless operators were not even Titanic crew, but rather contracted workers from a wireless company, made their role in the ship's operation quite unclear.

⁵ Captain Smith's seemingly casual attitude in increasing the speed on this day to a dangerous 22 knots or 41 kilometers per hour can then be partly explained by his ignorance of what lay ahead. But this only partly accounts for his actions, since the spring weather in Greenland was known to cause huge chunks of ice to break off from the glaciers. Captain Smith knew that these icebergs would float southward and had already acknowledged this danger by taking a more southerly route than at other times of the year. So why was the Titanic travelling at high speed when he knew, if not of the specific risk, at least of the general risk of icebergs in her path. As with the lack of coordination of the wireless messages, it was simply standard operating procedure at the time. Captain Smith was following the practices accepted on the North Atlantic, practices which had coincided with forty years of safe travel. He believed, wrongly as we now know, that the ship could turn or stop in time if an iceberg was sighted by the lookouts.

⁶ There were around two and a half hours between the time the Titanic rammed into the iceberg and its final submersion. In this time 705 people were loaded into the twenty lifeboats. There were 473 empty seats available on lifeboats while over 1,500 people drowned. These figures raise two important issues. Firstly, why were there not enough lifeboats to seat every passenger and crew member on board? And secondly, why were the lifeboats not full?

⁷ The Titanic had sixteen lifeboats and four collapsible boats which could carry just over half the number of people on board her maiden voyage and only a third of the Titanic's total capacity. Regulations for the number of lifeboats required were based on outdated British Board of Trade regulations written in 1894 for ships a quarter of the Titanic's size, and had never been revised. Under these requirements, the Titanic was only obliged to carry enough lifeboats to seat 962 people. At design meetings in 1910, the shipyard's managing director, Alexander Carlisle, had proposed that forty-eight lifeboats be installed on the Titanic, but the idea had been quickly rejected as too expensive. Discussion then turned to the ship's décor, and as Carlisle later described the incident … "we spent two hours discussing carpet for the first class cabins and fifteen minutes discussing lifeboats".

⁸ The belief that the Titanic was unsinkable was so strong that passengers and crew alike clung to the belief even as she was actually sinking. This attitude was not helped by Captain Smith, who had not acquainted his senior officers with the full situation. For the first hour after the collision, the majority of people aboard the Titanic, including senior crew, were not aware that she would sink, that there were insufficient lifeboats or that the nearest ship responding to the Titanic's distress calls would arrive two hours after she was on the bottom of the ocean. As a result, the officers in charge of loading the boats received a very halfhearted response to their early calls for women and children to board the lifeboats. People felt that they would be safer, and certainly warmer, aboard the Titanic than perched in a little boat in the North Atlantic Ocean. Not realizing the magnitude of the impending disaster themselves, the officers allowed several boats to be lowered only half full.

⁹ Procedures again were at fault, as an additional reason for the officers' reluctance to lower the lifeboats at full capacity was that they feared the lifeboats would buckle under the weight of 65 people. They had not been informed that the lifeboats had been fully tested prior to departure. Such procedures as assigning passengers and crew to lifeboats and lifeboat loading drills were simply not part of the standard operation of ships nor were they included in crew training at this time.

¹⁰ As the Titanic sank, another ship, believed to have been the Californian, was seen motionless less than twenty miles away. The ship failed to respond to the Titanic's eight distress rockets. Although the officers of the Californian tried to signal the Titanic with their flashing Morse lamp, they did not wake up their radio operator to listen for a distress call. At this time, communication at sea through wireless was new and the benefits not well appreciated, so the wireless on ships was often not operated around the clock. In the case of the Californian, the wireless operator slept unaware while 1,500 Titanic passengers and crew drowned only a few miles away.

¹¹ After the Titanic sank, investigations were held in both Washington and London. In the end, both inquiries decided that no one could be blamed for the sinking. However, they did address the fundamental safety issues which had contributed to the enormous loss of life. As a result, international agreements were drawn up to improve safety procedures at sea. The new regulations covered 24-hour wireless operation, crew training, proper lifeboat drills, lifeboat capacity for all on board and the creation of an international ice patrol.

Source: April 15, 1912. The sinking of the Titanic. (n. d.). *Titanic Facts*. Retrieved September 22, 2020. From http://www.titanic-facts.com/1912-the-sinking-of-the-titanic.html.

Post-reading activity

Task A | Reading Comprehension Strategy: Scanning

What is scanning?

> **Scanning** is a form of speed-reading. When you scan the text, you're looking at headings, scanning the body of the piece for any frequently used words or concept while reviewing the thesis of the piece and attempting to gain a general idea of the piece's argument.

English Reading for Academic Purposes 1A

Exercise

Scan the text and answer the questions below using **no more than three words** or **only one number**.

1. When did the Titanic sink?

   _____

2. How many warnings of icebergs did the Titanic's wireless operators receive?

   _____

3. How many empty seats were available when over 1,500 people drowned?

   _____

Task B | Language Spotlight: Summary completion

How to approach summary completion

◇ The input for this type of question will be a summary of all or part of the reading text. The summary will contain a number of gaps. All of the information in the summary will be contained in the reading text, although the words used will be different.

◇ You will also be provided with a list of words to use to fill the gaps. There will be more words than gaps. These words have been chosen so that only one word will be suitable for each gap (the answer) but other words may appear suitable (distracters). Your task is to complete the summary using one word from the list for each gap.

Exercise

Complete the summary below by using the following ten words. Make changes when necessary.

| iceberg | severity | radio | survivor | bulk |
| collide | unaware | quivering | grave | catastrophic |

Even though crew members were desperately trying to turn the ship in the other direction, when the ship _____ with the berg a massive rip was torn parallel across the ship's _____. The Titanic sinking began almost immediately, as the ship began to take on water.

126 | Unit 5 Uncovered History

Surprisingly, many of the passengers remained _____ of this fact. Some passengers reported hearing and feeling a strange _____ in the ship; however, they did not attribute this to any potential problem and went on about their business.

Others had seen the _____ has it passed their window and hurriedly donned dressing gowns and robes, anxious to discover whether or not they had truly hit the berg. At first, passengers were assured that there would only be a slight delay and were given no indication of the true _____ of the situation.

Passengers located at strategic points in the ship already knew the devastating truth however: the Titanic was sinking and sinking fast. An SOS was sent out to neighboring ships. The Carpathia picked up the ship's distress call and _____ back to let the ship's crew know they were on their way. It would be too late, however. By the time the Carpathia arrived, all that remained of the Titanic was a handful of lifeboats filled with shocked _____.

Since the ship sank to her watery _____, almost one hundred years ago, a number of theories have been put forth to explain how in the year of 1912 the sinking of the Titanic could have occurred. Some theories suggest that had the ship's crew not attempted to turn the ship in the opposite direction of the iceberg and instead took the blow head-on, the collision would not have resulted in such _____ disaster.

Find more on website: https://www.titanic-facts.com/1912-the-sinking-of-the-titanic.html

Task C | Vocabulary Practice: Words related to describing a cruise

Match the following words with definitions.

crew   lifeboat   captain   unsinkable   iceberg

1. the men and women who work on a vehicle (ship, aircraft, etc.)
2. a strong sea boat designed to rescue people from a sinking ship
3. the naval officer in command of a military ship
4. incapable of being sunk
5. a large mass of ice floating at sea; usually broken off of a polar glacier

Task D | Critical Thinking: Summary and comparison

Discuss with your partner and think about the following questions. You may take notes in the table.

1. What can you learn from the tragedy of Titanic shipwreck?
2. Compare this article with the Movie *Titanic*. What can you learn from it?

Notes

Glossary of Unit 5

Reading 1

aesthetic
adj. concerning or characterized by an appreciation of beauty or good taste
e. g. Poetry for him is simply a shorthand for literature that has aesthetic value.

pantomime
n. a performance using gestures and body movements without words
e. g. Before this I saw *The Witches*, a pantomime, I felt composed, serene, and happy.

impersonation
n. a representation of a person that is exaggerated for comic effect
e. g. How did the impersonation of Mao effect the Mao doubles' own life?

rhythmical
adj. recurring with measured regularity
e. g. Clapper talk is rhythmical, so it's easy to memorize.

envision
v. to imagine; to conceive of; to see in one's mind
e. g. In the future we envision a federation of companies.

antecedent
n. a thing or an event that exists or comes before another, and may have influenced it
e. g. The cavemen lived in a period of history antecedent to written records

objectify
v. to make impersonal or present as an object
e. g. It is so pervasive a dimension that it is difficult to objectify in spatial terms and difficult to consider apart from oneself.

imitative
adj. not genuine; imitating something
e. g. Babies of eight to twelve months are generally highly imitative.

efficacious
adj. effective
e. g. This medicine is highly efficacious.

Reading 2

crew
n. all the people working on a ship, a plane, etc.
e. g. The British crew are no longer the lame ducks of the Olympic team.

lifeboat
n. a strong sea boat designed to rescue people from a sinking ship
e. g. The power plant of the lifeboat had been rigged to explode.

captain
n. the naval officer in command of a military ship
e. g. If the captain has a family or any absorbing concernment of that sort.

unsinkable
adj. incapable of being sunk

e. g. The supposedly unsinkable ship hit an iceberg.

iceberg

n. a large mass of ice floating at sea, usually broken off a polar glacier

e. g. The supposedly unsinkable ship hit an iceberg.

acquaint

v. to be familiar with

e. g. You will first need to acquaint yourself with the filing system.

ram

v. to hit each other

e. g. Two passengers were injured when their taxi was rammed from behind by a bus.

collision

n. an accident in which two vehicles or people crash into each other

e. g. His car was in collision with a motorbike.

Extended Reading

Five Guesses on Emperor Qin Shihuang's Tomb

Qin Shihuang holds a central place in Chinese history for being the first emperor who united the country. He is also well known for his part in the construction of the spectacular Great Wall and his splendid terracotta army.

To ensure his rule in the afterlife, this emperor commanded more than 700,000 conscripts from all parts of the country to build him a grand mausoleum as luxurious as any of the palaces he had in mortal life. Legend says that numerous treasures were placed in the tomb.

As time passed, no one knew exactly what was put in the grand palace. Recently, Guo Zhikun, a specialist in the history of the Qin (221 BC – 206 BC) and Han (206 BC – 220 AD) dynasties, gave a press conference in Xi'an. He disclosed his academic research results focusing on the Mausoleum of Emperor Qin Shihuang, making bold guesses about the mysterious tomb complex that fascinates the whole world.

Guess 1: How tall was the tomb mound?

According to Guo, the Mausoleum of Emperor Qin Shihuang is actually composed of two parts: the tomb mound, a hillock above the tomb, and the underground palace, the chamber containing the emperor's coffin.

Most historical records indicate that the original tomb mound was 115 meters in height and 2,076 meters in girth. Exposed to the wind and sun for thousands of years, the mound has been greatly weathered down. The current girth is 1,390 meters, and the base of the mound covers an area of 120,750 square meters.

There has been a decades-long argument about why the mound's height dropped so sharply in recent years. Guo said that most people attributed it to the erosion from wind and rain and to man-made changes. However, another opinion has emerged recently.

According to Duan Qingbo who leads the archaeological team at the mausoleum, the height of 115 meters recorded in most historical documents was just a figure copied down from the original blueprint. It is believed that the construction was left unfinished due to a nationwide uprising of peasants. After the emperor's corpse was placed in the chamber, the tomb mound project began. Later, about half of the laborers were transferred to the construction site of another palace building. When the peasant army approached the Mausoleum of Emperor Qin Shihuang, the second emperor of the dynasty, who had taken the throne from his dead father, hastily organized the remaining workers on the construction site to fight against the rebels. No more soil were added onto the hillock later.

Guess 2: How many gates does the underground palace have?

Opinions also differ on how many gates the underground palace contains. Some said there were two, one made of stone and the other of bronze. Others said that there were six, because Emperor Qin Shihuang had always considered the number "six" auspicious.

How many gates does the underground palace have then? After reading through piles of ancient documents, Guo Zhikun said that the exact number was recorded clearly in *Records of the Historian*, a great historical book written by Sima Qian. In it, the author wrote, "When the emperor died, he was placed in the underground palace. Then, the middle gate was closed and the outer gate was shut down. All workmen were entombed. No one escaped."

Guo explained that the emperor's coffin and all his burial articles were placed inside the middle gate. When the palace was shut down, workmen were busy working in it. Within seconds, however, they were entombed along with the emperor and became burial sacrifices themselves.

From Sima Qian's description, Guo inferred that the underground palace had three gates: an outer gate, a middle gate and an unmentioned inner gate. In addition, in Sima Qian's record, the middle gate was "closed", which meant it had two planks, and the outer gate was "shut down", which meant it slide down vertically. Guo believed the middle door was locked automatically once it was closed. It was designed deliberately to prevent any breakthrough from inside or any invasion from outside. Besides, Guo guessed the unmentioned inner gate had the same mechanism as the middle one and the three gates were located on a straight line.

Guess 3: How many treasures lie buried?

The tomb of Emperor Qin Shihuang was filled with fine vessels, precious stones and other rarities according to Sima Qian's record. Liu Xiang, another famous scholar before Sima Qian, wrote in one of his passages, "Since antiquity, no one has ever been buried in such a luxurious manner as Emperor Qin Shihuang."

All the sketchy but intriguing words made us curious about the mysterious wealth buried in the magnificent underground palace. In *Records of the Historian*, one can find descriptions about a golden wild goose, pearls and jade. But what else lies down there? In the late 1980s, a large bronze chariot equipped with life-size horses was unearthed outside the west wall of the underground palace of Emperor Qin Shihuang. These elaborately decorated burial articles fascinated the world about the treasures hidden in the emperor's tomb chamber.

"Emperor Qin Shihuang was fond of music. He must have all kinds of musical instruments buried with him," guessed Guo. Recently, a pit for sacrifices was found between the inner wall and outer wall of the tomb complex. Covering 600 square meters, the pit was 40 meters wide from east to west and 15 meters long from north to south. Most of the articles excavated were pottery figures of courtiers, musicians and acrobats. In recent years, a variety of traditional Chinese musical instruments, such as Bianzhong (bronze chimes), were unearthed. Guo felt confident that the underground palace must have a whole collection of musical instruments. Besides, Guo guessed that there might be many valuable ancient books in addition to treasures and jewels.

Guess 4: Does the automatic-shooting crossbows function well?

Ancient Chinese tended to bury treasures with them. Not surprisingly, tomb robbery was once rampant throughout the country. To prevent outside invasions, Emperor Qin Shihuang ordered a full range of precautions. It is said that besides poisonous mercury, booby traps with automatically ejected arrows were installed in the tomb chamber to deter would-be robbers. Anyone who dared to break in would certainly die a violent death.

However, all those alleged lethal weapons have been buried under earth for thousands of years. Would they still function adequately now? Most people believe that the crossbows would still shoot arrows if they are triggered. Guo also agreed so after he carefully studied ancient smelting technology recorded in historical books.

In a modern test, a coating of chromate was found on the surface of weapons excavated along with the terracotta warriors. This coating served to make bronze weapons rust-resistant. Thus, it is highly likely that the automatic crossbows may function well even after thousands of years.

Guo speculated that these crossbows were the first automatic burglar-proof devices in the world. "Craftsmen were ordered to fix up these crossbows in such a way so that any thief breaking in would be shot." He quoted a line in *Records of the Historian* to support his prediction.

Guess 5: Is the corpse of Emperor Qin Shihuang well preserved?

Although it is widely believed that the underground palace has not been disturbed in past years, some people hold the opinion that the emperor's body had putrefied.

According to historical records, the emperor died during an inspection tour. It was summer so the body couldn't be kept for long. In fact, records state that the body had started to stink even before it was carried back to the capital.

In one of his works, Guo pointed out that it is possible the emperor's corpse might be relatively well preserved. He had three reasons supporting his assumption. First, during the Qin era, it was common practice among aristocrats to put mercury in their tombs to prevent corpses from decaying. Second, when the emperor died, all prominent officials were accompanying him, along with an imperial doctor with superb medical skills who was summoned to his deathbed. Third, modern tests on the soil of the tomb mound show unusually high concentrations of mercury. Guo pointed out all these conditions indicate the possibility of preservation for his body.

Guo: All the guesses have to be testified by archaeological finds.

At the press conference, Guo's new book, *Guesses on the Underground Palace of Qin Mausoleum*, was introduced to the public. "When I wrote this book, I consulted scores of famous archaeologists via letters, E-mails or face-to-face communications. They all gave me tremendous help." Guo Zhikun said that his assumptions were based on the results of previous research. If they turn out to be correct, the credit should be given to all scholars engaged in this field.

As technology advances, maybe one day we can open the grand palace and discover all the answers to these questions.

Source: Chen, X. (2007, October 24). Five guesses on Emperor Qin Shihuang's tomb. *China. org. cn.* Retrieved September 22, 2020, from http://www.china.org.cn/english/culture.

Unit 6

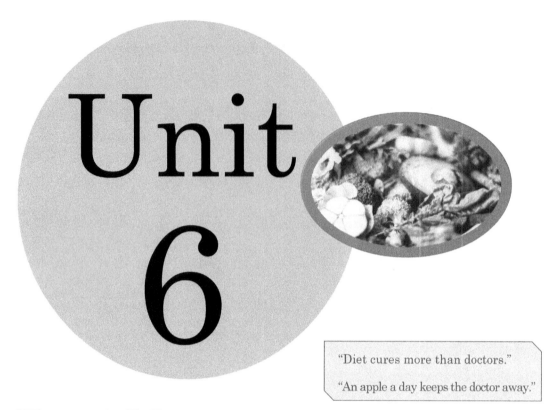

"Diet cures more than doctors."

"An apple a day keeps the doctor away."

Food Matters

In this unit you are going to think on how to eat heathy meals. You will have a further look at the topic of diet-related diseases, especially about obesity. You will further extend your vocabulary of various foods. And there is also a focus on the expressions for describing our eating experience. Also there are opportunities for word formation practice of prefixes and suffixes.

Meanwhile, you will learn skimming skill for finding main ideas, which is now so often used in reading comprehension. Features of research reports will be covered in this unit, and you may have to use it in the academic research with your classmates, lecturers and other staff during your further studies. In this part, you will practice your academic writing skills, and will also learn to identify language features of reports.

By the end of this unit, you will be able to:	
SKILL	TASK
increase general knowledge about the current issues of diet food and critically consider it globally	• Speaking • Tasks A, B
extend vocabulary related to food	• Speaking • Task A
know how to measure obesity	• Speaking • Task B
know 3 types of writing	• Reading 1 • Pre-reading activity • Task A
know skimming skill for main ideas	• Reading 1 • Pre-reading activity • Task A • Post-reading activity • Task A
have some knowledge of prefixes mal-, over- & suffixes -ness, -hood, -sick, -ful, -aholic	• Reading 1 • Post-reading activity • Task B
know how to describe food	• Reading 1 • Task C
do critical thinking about eating healthy food	• Reading 1 • Task D
know features of research reports	• Reading 2 • Post-reading activity • Task A
increase general knowledge about academic writing style	• Reading 2 • Task B
identify language features of reports	• Reading 2 • Task C
debate on selected topic	• Reading 2 • Task D

SPEAKING

Task A | Orientation: Food in Our Lives

Consider some issues regarding healthy food and junk food in your daily life. Do you like junk food or fast food? Do you know how eating junk food or fast food in the long term could cause harm to your health? It is a fact that diet-related disease, which is a global problem, is the biggest killer in the United States. Specifically, people in Mexico, Australia, the United Kingdom, Germany, India, China or other countries also suffer from obesity and poor health.

1. Ask your partner the following questions:
    1) Can you name any healthy food?
    2) Can you name any junk food?
    3) Can you name any fast food?
    4) What is your favorite food? Is it healthy food or junk food?
    5) Do you know any diet-related diseases?
    6) Do you know the harm of diet-related diseases to the body?
    7) Compare the quantitative trend of obesity among adolescents in your country with the trend in the United States.
    8) Do you know what indicators can be used to measure obesity?
    9) Do you know how to keep fit? And what kinds of food can keep us healthy?
        – organic food
        – balanced diet
        – vegetarian dishes
        – fruit
        – high-quality protein
        – etc.

2. Within a group discussion, please take notes on other students' ideas of the above questions by completing the table below.

Listing main ideas	Giving reasons or details

SPEAKING Task B | How to Measure Obesity

1. Here we have a piece of news about China's waistline. Let's listen to it and find more information of how to measure obesity. Meanwhile, you need to finish *minutes* that we have already learned in Unit 2 during listening.

also known as protocols or notes
(as a summary or recommendation)

China's waistline is expanding
—according to a new (1)_____ report

The document, (2)_____ Wednesday by the National Health Commission. → over half of Chinese adults are (3)_____, raising concerns about health issues (4)_____ with obesity.

Body mass index (BMI)
— a person's (5)_____ in kilograms divided by their (6)_____ height in meters.
— is the most common (7)_____ criterion for measuring obesity.

According to the World Health Organization, a person with a BMI of over (8)_____ is considered overweight, or (9)_____ if it's over 30.

2. In pairs, look at the minutes above and try to figure out the answers.

3. After that, according to the measurement method in the news, please measure your own BMI to see whether you are in a healthy condition.

You may use a learner's dictionary to help you understand it better.

How does a person become obese?
— Obesity is caused by energy imbalance. Obesity is a condition in which the body stores large, unhealthy amounts of fat.

Reference: TED-What is obesity-Mia Nacamulli

1. With a partner or in groups, discuss the following questions:
   1) Obesity harms health, do you agree or disagree?
   2) Think how a person becomes obese.
   3) List as many kinds of triggers of being obese as you can.
   4) List as many advantages or disadvantages of being obese as you can.
   5) For each, give an example to support your argument.

2. Here, look at the following *types of writing*, try to choose one to guide your discussion.

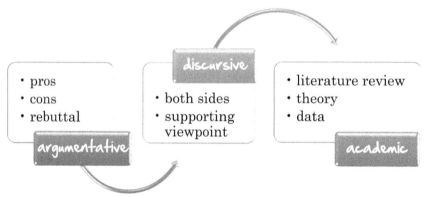

◌ Instructions

1) Try to use the *note formats* you have learned in Unit 2 to find your main viewpoints.
2) Make an essay outline before you begin to write or speak.
3) You should give a topic sentence for each point.
4) You should give more specific supporting information and evidences about that point.
5) You should keep your points clear, specific, and arguable.

3. Discuss in groups, and write down your drafts below.

_____
_____
_____
_____
_____
_____
_____
_____
_____
_____
_____
_____
_____
_____
_____
_____
_____
_____
_____
_____
_____
_____

The text you will read on the next page is an article citing data and information from VOA Learning English and HealthHearty.com, *A Health Report*. Read about childhood obesity statistics in this text, and get to know how acute this problem has become in the whole world. Understanding the gravity of the issue can help us to become more sensitive regarding obesity as a medical condition. Read the text and find key challenges and solutions and write them on the *minutes* at the end of it.

A Health Report

—From VOA Learning English & HealthHearty.com

1. According to the World Health Organization (WHO), most of the world's population lives in countries where obesity, rather than malnourishment (as a factor), causes death. The threat of obesity has become a major health concern for adults and children alike, and has heightened in the past few decades in the US. It has become a striking reality in the US society, and has only worsened over the last 30 years. Childhood obesity statistics are alarming, and they have compelled the government and health agencies to focus on health reforms and create an awareness about this grave medical condition. Before plunging into childhood obesity data collected from various sources, knowing the cause of childhood obesity is vital to treat this disease.

Causes

2. Statistics related to obesity in children have established a close relation between unhealthy eating habits and the increase in extra body fat. In fact, poor eating habits are cited to be one of the major causes of childhood obesity. Francesco Branca is the director of the WHO Department of Nutrition for Health and Development. He says people are eating manufactured or processed food more often, and it often has a high sugar, fat and salt content. With fast foods as an integral and unavoidable part of dietary habits, it's not surprising to observe a significant rise in the number of children suffering from issues related to their weight. Who should be blamed for the health crisis assuming an endemic proportion in kids all across the US? First and foremost, it is sad to note that some parents are careless, or rather they have no time for their kids to provide them cooked meals and educate them on healthy eating.

3. Certainly, causes and effects of childhood obesity need to be understood with the help of an expert nutritionist, and fostering the habit of eating healthy foods should be developed in kids. While unhealthy eating leads as the major cause of obesity, there are several social, behavioral, and genetic causes

of obesity, which must be kept in mind for understanding the nuisances of obesity from a larger perspective.

Statistics

[4] As per the reports published on the official website of the Centers for Disease Control and Prevention (CDC), in September 2014, approximately 17% (or 12.7 million) of children and adolescents aged 2 – 19 years are obese. Obesity in children has become a challenging issue for doctors and parents across the US. To understand the current situation closely, consider the statistics published by the CDC to show the gravity of this problem—the percentage of children aged 6 – 11 years in the United States who were obese increased from 7% in 1980 to nearly 18% in 2012. Similarly, the percentage of adolescents aged 12 – 19 years who were obese increased from 5% to nearly 21% over the same period. Besides the CDC, there are several NGOs and medical institutions working relentlessly to spread awareness about child obesity. The following statistics have been compiled from several resources, and are just aimed to spread more awareness about the current state of childhood obesity around the world.

- The instances of childhood obesity in the US have risen 3 times in the last 30 years.
- Almost 25% obese adults were obese in their childhood.
- As per research by WHO, in Africa countries, the number of overweight or obese children is two times as high as it was 20 years ago.
- BMI data from 200 countries show that the child obesity rate has risen from 4% in 1975 to 18% in 2016. Researchers pointed out that although childhood obesity rates are stable in the United States, obesity rates continue to rise in countries in East Asia, the Middle East, North Africa and South Asia.
- As per research by CDC, the number of children meeting the dietary guidelines in the US is very less, just about 40%.
- Almost 30% of kids eat some type of fast food every day of the year. If the consumption of fast food is at such a high rate, it's not surprising if children are at a risk of getting obese.

- In the US, a trend has been observed where children spend more time in front of the idiot box and computers, eating fast foods, and stuffing chocolates and snacks all the time, than in sports and games. This has made them vulnerable to obesity.
- The WHO also says people are gaining weight because of city lifestyles. They travel in cars or other vehicles more than on foot, and they take part in few physical activities in general.

5   Children with problems of obesity are bound to suffer from other problems like depression and social anxiety disorders. This is due to the fact that obese children may feel shy and hesitant to approach others due to their weight issues. Being overweight or obese can cause many serious health problems later in life, including diabetes, heart disease, stroke, and cancer.

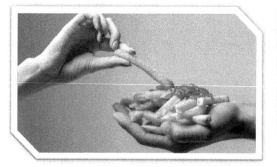

Global Solutions

6   It is indicated that lowering obesity rate is especially complex in countries that also deal with higher rate of infectious disease. The WHO has some basic solutions for individuals and countries.
- People should lower in-take of fat, sugar, salt and processed food, and then eat more fruit and vegetables, and also increase physical activity. These actions are especially important for children.
- WHO experts suggest mothers should breastfeed their babies for at least the first six months of life if possible.

- The report is calling for policymakers to find ways to make healthy food more available at home and school, especially in poorer families and communities.
- Government should concern providing vitamin for children. And educational campaigns about problems linked to obesity would also help.
- Government policies should deal with how food is marketed to children.
- Food manufactures must balance quality and taste with the dangers of sugar, fat and salt.

7   Fast-paced lifestyle in America is a contributing factor for increasing obesity in people who don't get sufficient time to even cook a meal at home. Children growing up in such homes automatically rely on junk foods for eating, and so do the parents. Busy lifestyle, hectic work schedule, and prosperity in the US have made fast food one of the biggest businesses in packaged food industry. The significant jump in the childhood obesity statistics over the past few years is a warning bell for all of us, and we must take steps to put a check on increasing menace of obesity. Spreading awareness about obesity and its negative implications through childhood obesity prevention tips can go a long way in inculcating and monitoring healthy eating habits in children.

Post-reading activity

Task A | Reading Comprehension Strategy: Skimming for main ideas

Minutes

Key challenges	Details
– Challenge 1 ✓ US	Major health concern Obesity rate in 2014: 2 – 19 yrs ____% 　　　　　　　in 2012: 6 – 11 yrs ____% 　　　　　　　in 2012: 12 – 19 yrs ____% 　　　　　　　in 1980: 6 – 11 yrs ____% 　　　　　　　in 1980: 12 – 19 yrs ____% Number of children meeting the dietary guidelines: ____% Consumption of fast food among children: _____%
– Challenge 2 ✓ Africa	Number of overweight or obese children _____ times as high as it was 20 years ago
– Challenge 3 ✓ 200 countries	Child obesity rate In 1975: _____% In 2016: _____% Obesity rates continue to rise in _____, _____, _____, and _____, but be stable in _____.
– Challenge 4 ✓ Unhealthy food	Manufactured or processed food contains 　– _____ 　– _____ 　– _____ Junk food like: _____ _____
– Challenge 5 ✓ City lifestyle	People 　– _____ 　– _____
– Challenge 6 ✓ Serious diet-related diseases	Health problems such as 　– _____　　– _____ 　– _____　　– _____ 　– _____　　– _____
– Challenge 7 ✓ Lower obesity rate	Basic solutions 　– Lower your in-take of _____ 　– Eat more _____ 　– Increase _____ 　– Mothers should _____ 　– Government should 　　_____ 　　_____ 　– Food manufactures must _____

How to identify the implied main idea

Step 1: Analyze the article title, and read the passage of text.
Step 2: Ask this question to yourself while reading: "What do the contents described in each paragraph of this article have in common?"
Step 3: Find out the common point of view between all the details of the article and the author's attitude of this point of view.
 - Tips: we can look for sentences or paragraphs at the beginning or end of the article, or sentences that appear repeatedly in the article.

Step 4: Write a short summary to clarify the above common point and the author's views on this point of view.

Exercises

1. Please identify the main idea from the above health report and answer the questions that follow.

   1) From the introductory paragraph, can you say what is the main problem the report will talk about in the text?

   2) According to the report, is the obesity rate of children in the US declining or increasing? How do we understand this trend?

   3) Can you draw a graph based on the data depicted in the health report above?

   4) What are the possible causes of the trend you drew in Question 3?

   5) Why is lowering obesity rate a challenge?

   6) There are several critical solutions introduced in this report. What's your opinion of these solutions? Are these solutions effective for the mentioned challenges?

2. Skimming race

   Read the question below. Then skim the report again. Put your hand up when you finish.

   Which organizational pattern does the report follow?
   [a] Introduction → data & facts → reasons → problems → solutions
   [b] Introduction → problems → data & facts → reasons → solutions
   [c] Introduction → reasons → data & facts → problems → solutions

3. Find the best title for the health report above _____
   [a] Obese Children in African Countries
   [b] Battles on Childhood Obesity
   [c] Causes for Overweight and Obesity
   [d] How to Lower Obesity Rate

Task B | Language Spotlight: Prefixes mal-, over- & suffixes -ness, -hood, -sick, -ful, -aholic

Prefixes	Usual meaning	Examples
mal-	bad, ill, poorly, wrong, evil	malnourishment
over-	above, across, beyond, excessive	overweight
Suffixes	Usual meaning	Examples
-ness	word-forming element denoting action, quality or state, attached to an adjective or past participle to form an abstract noun	awareness
-hood	word-forming element meaning "state or condition of being"	childhood
-sick	making someone ill or unhappy because of a particular emotion	homesick
-ful	full of a particular quality; providing something with a particular amount	useful, mouthful
-aholic	someone who likes something a lot, or who is unable to stop doing something	chocoholic

Exercises

1. Form new words with the following words and the prefixes/suffixes in the table.

Column A	Newly-formed words	Meaning
air		
car		
sea		
spoon		
alcohol		
cloud		
food		

Column B	Newly-formed words	Meaning
help		
whelm		
burden		
bear		

Column C	Newly-formed words	Meaning
shop		
work		
effective		
girl		
adult		

2. Answer the questions with the words you formed in Exercise 1.

What's the word for?

(1) Uncomfortable feeling when someone is on the boat?
(2) Someone who likes shopping a lot?
(3) Someone who was charged with too many tasks?
(4) The period of a female person's life during which she is a girl?
(5) The period of time in your life after your physical growth has stopped and you are fully developed?
(6) Someone who is addicted to drinking in excess?

English Reading for Academic Purposes 1B

Task C | Vocabulary Practice: Describing food

1. Please listen to Helen's programme and name the food you can't stand.

Seafood Culture

Given that the UK is surrounded by water, it's natural to assume that creatures from the sea are part of the staple diet. However, it appears that this is not the case. British fishmongers seem to have far fewer varieties of seafood on offer than one would expect.

What is the explanation for this? What do people think of seafood?

Here we have a recording of Helen Hu's talking to the British public and find out what they really think about seafood. And then finish the form below. (From BBC "Ask about Britain")

Jo
- Reason 1:
- Reason 2:

Historical reason
- In middle ages, oysters were the most _____ food that people could eat.
- Oyster can be very _____. Lots of people _____ because of oysters. People tend to _____ eat seafood.

Sarah
- _____: we're not _____ to seafood when we're children. We don't see it very often.
- Seafood can be quite _____ to eat; there're shells and bones to take out. And a lot of people can't be bothered with that.

2. According to the health report above, please make an inference of the reasons why people like to eat unhealthy food.

Taste	Texture	Other reasons

3. This section is all about food and expressions we can use to describe our eating experience.
   What do the following words mean? Put them in the correct column of the table below.

bland	*delish*	*delectable*	*delightful*	*disgusting*
flavorful	*flavorless*	*finger-licking*	*mouthful*	*mouthwatering*
scrumptious	*tasteless*	*tasty*	*taste funny*	*taste horrible*
taste off	*yummy*	*unappetizing*		

Taste good	Taste bad

4. Using your shared knowledge or a dictionary, decide which of the words in the table:
   a) have the suffix -ful
   b) have the suffix -less

Task D | Critical Thinking: Debate on "Eating healthy food is good for our health"

1. Do you think that eating healthy food is good for our health?
2. Why? Or why not?
3. What else do you think are possible solutions to lower the obesity rate?

Yes	No

READING & CRITICAL THINKING

Reading 2

Pre-reading activity

1. Have you ever read a tourism magazine or a newspaper written in English?
2. If yes, what kind of magazines or newspapers have you read?
3. Discuss with your partner, share your reading experiences with them.

Tourism magazines or newspapers you have read	No reading experience
	Please take notes of the main points of other students' reading experiences.

English Reading for Academic Purposes 1B

4. Words and word groups list
   ① First, you are to scan the excerpt "How Might Exercise Affect Our Food Choices and Our Weight?" on the next page for the following nouns, noun phrases/groups and nominalizations contained in the text.
   ② Second, please locate the words in the following sheet, and write the number of the paragraph in which the words are firstly mentioned in the text.

Words and word groups list

a. Paragraph 1	novice exercisers
b.	dietitian
c.	volunteers
d.	study participants
e.	overweight or obese
f.	little alteration
g.	less desire of
h.	showed less "wanting"
i.	fewer instances of
j.	fattening foods
k.	high-fat foods
l.	binge eating
m.	susceptibility to overconsume
n.	favorable outcome
o.	the same drive

154 | Unit 6 Food Matters

How Might Exercise Affect Our Food Choices and Our Weight?

By Gretchen Reynolds

Published on Feb. 26, 2020   The New York Times

This excerpt is from the original article on *The New York Times* website (nytimes.com).

The New York Times is an American daily newspaper based in New York City with a worldwide readership. Founded in 1851, the *Times* has won 130 Pulitzer Prizes, and has long been regarded within the industry as a national "newspaper of record". It is ranked the 18th in the world by circulation and the 3rd in the US (from Wikipedia).

From Wikipedia http://en.volupedia.org/wiki/The_New_York_Times

Men and women who started an exercise program no longer found high-calorie, fatty foods quite so irresistible, a recent study found. How was this study conducted? What does it enlighten for our way of life?

1   Taking up exercise could alter our feelings about food in surprising and beneficial ways, according to a compelling new study of exercise and eating. The study finds that novice exercisers start to experience less desire for fattening foods, a change that could have long-term implications for weight control.

2   The study also shows, though, that different people respond quite differently to the same exercise routine and the same foods, underscoring the complexities of the relationship between exercise, eating and fat loss.

3   So, for the new study, which was published in November in *Medicine & Science in Sports & Exercise*, researchers at the University of Leeds in England and other institutions decided to ask a group of sedentary men and women about how they felt about food and to begin working out.

4   The researchers wound up recruiting 61 volunteers, most of them middle-aged and inactive; all were overweight or obese. The study participants completed detailed questionnaires and online tests of their food preferences and behaviors, picking, for instance, between rapid-fire, on-screen pictures of different foods and also answering questions about bingeing on food and whether they found it hard to not overeat.

5   Fifteen of the volunteers then were asked to continue with their normal lives as a control group, while the other 46 began exercising, working out on exercise machines at a university facility five times a week for about 45 to 60 minutes or until they had burned about 500 calories per session. They continued this training for 12 weeks, eating as they liked at home.

6   The men and women in the control group also showed little alteration in their feelings about food. But the exercisers' reactions to pictures of and questions about high-calorie, fatty foods were new. They no longer found them quite so irresistible. In psychological terms, they showed less "wanting" for the most fattening foods.

7   Interestingly, their scores on measures of "liking", or how much they expected to enjoy those same foods, remained unchanged and strong. They still felt that they would enjoy a cookie but did not feel quite the same drive to seek one out. They also reported fewer instances of recent binge eating.

8   In addition to making us healthier, "exercise might improve food reward and eating behavior traits linked to the susceptibility to overconsume," says Kristine Beaulieu, a dietitian who led the new study. In other words, working out for a period of time could nudge us to rethink the kinds of foods we want to eat.

⁹ "People still liked high-fat foods to the same extent," after four months of training, Dr. Beaulieu points out, "but they wanted to eat them less, which we view as a favorable outcome."

¹⁰ For now, the study reinforces the idea that exercise should be part of our efforts to manage our weight.

Please go to *The New York Times* official website to see the full article.

Source: Reynolds, G. (2020, February 26). How exercise might affect our food choices, and our weight. *The New York Times*. Retrieved May 20, 2021, from https://www.nytimes.com/2020/02/26/well/move/how-exercise-might-affect-our-food-choices-and-our-weight.amp.html.

Post-reading activity

Task A | Reading Comprehension Strategy: Features of research reports

1. Read the excerpt again. With a partner, analyze the **news lead** of the excerpt in the following ways:

   [a] What is the theme in the first paragraph?

   [b] Where might it be written?

   [c] What occupation might the author do?

   [d] Who is it written for?

   [e] What is the author's bias or opinion?

Research reports

In college, a research report is a very difficult assignment that reports on the findings of a research project or alternatively scientific observations on or about a subject. Many university courses include mini research projects, and lecturers will grade the students based on the results (mainly research reports) of the team members' collaboration. There are two major kinds of academic research:

★ **Primary research:**

It is the process of collecting and investigating primary data. Primary data is the type of data that researchers collect to answer the question at hand. In other words, it is also called raw data, which refers to data directly observed or collected from first-hand experience. Technically, the researchers "own" the data. Some common kinds of primary research methods include:

- Experimental research
- Survey research
- Observation

★ **Secondary research:**

It is also called desk research, which is the process of collecting and investigating existing data. Secondary data can be found in university libraries and on the Internet. Books, government publications, periodicals and electronic databases, magazines and newspapers are also important sources of secondary data. Some common kinds of secondary research methods include:

- Library research
- Internet-based research

Please go to http://en.volupedia.org/wiki/Research_report for more information.

2. With a partner, answer questions below. It may be helpful for you to recall the research you did in your previous studies—such as experimental research in science and engineering courses.
   [a] What kind of academic research does this article (Reading 2) belong to?
   [b] Which research method would you choose? And why?
   [c] What are the similarities and differences between primary research and secondary research? Check your answers and complete the table below.

Key Differences Between Primary Research and Secondary Research

Primary research	Secondary research
Research is conducted _____ hand to obtain data. Researchers "_____" the data collected.	Research is based on data collected from _____ researches.
Primary research is based on _____ data.	Secondary research is based on _____ data.
The data collected are in line with the needs of the researcher, and are generated specifically for the research questions for a specific purpose.	Data may or may not meet the requirements of researchers, because they are already done by other people.
Researchers have complete control over the research process, and will be deeply involved in the research project to collect _____ data.	Secondary research is a quick process as data are already available. Researchers could collect the relevant data they need through published periodicals, books, reports, etc.
Such research is often more time-consuming and costly. Generally speaking, before starting primary research, secondary research should be carried out to determine what information is not yet available.	Contrasted with primary research, secondary research is fast and easy. A common practice for researchers is to conduct a _____ research before primary research in order to filter data and information.

3. Check the components of research reports by looking at the table below.

Components of Research Reports

The components of the research report may vary with the purpose of the research, but the main part of the report remains the same.

Components	Notes
i. Title	To clarify your research topic.
ii. Abstract	It contains the main points of the research report, as well as an overview of the research, and it is 1 – 2 paragraphs in length. It records the main content of the report concisely and accurately.

(Continuous)

Components	Notes
iii. Introduction	It may include - a clear definition of the topic and the purpose of the report; - relevant background information of the topic; - literature review of the previous related researches and their limitations (citations are needed); - precise hypothesis and research questions; - explanation of the outline of the report.
iv. Methodology	To describe the methodology completely, including the means how the data were collected, and the technical means to verify the authenticity of the data.
v. Results	An overview of the data of your experiments or a summary of the findings with figures and tables, if necessary.
vi. Discussion	It may include - detailed explanation of the findings; - indication of the authenticity of the statistics; - evaluation of the hypothesis; - comments on the findings.
vii. Conclusion	It may include - summary of the key findings in the report; - explanation of the unexpected results; - possible implications; - limitations of the work covered by your report; - future research directions.
viii. Reference List	To list all literature cited in your paper. And be aware of plagiarism.

Task B | Language Spotlight: Academic writing style

1. Read the excerpt of "How Might Exercise Affect Our Food Choices and Our Weight?" again and discuss how to make your writing more formal and academic.
2. Discuss the writing style of common types of report:

Notes	
i. Choice of words	
ii. Grammatical structures	
iii. Personal pronouns & tone	
iv. Tense or verb forms	
v. Citations	
vi. Organization of report	
vii. Logic of the paper	
viii. ...	

3. Read the excerpt of "How Might Exercise Affect Our Food Choices and Our Weight?" again, and complete the table below. And pay attention to the way how the experimental data were written and discussed in the Reading 2.

Experiment and Result (Reading 2)

How many volunteers	Features	Preparation
61	middle-aged and inactive overweight or obese	
Group 1 (volunteers)	Requirement	Result
Group 2 (volunteers)	Requirement	Result

Task C | Vocabulary Practice: Identifying language features of reports

1. With a partner, examine the examples of hypernyms and hyponyms first and give hyponyms to the following hypernyms in the table below, which tend to be used in academic writing.

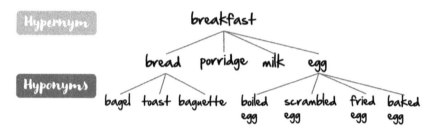

Hypernyms	Hyponyms
Expressions of purpose	aim, purpose, goal, motive, in order to, for the sake of ...
Explanation verbs	analyze, explain, explicate, interpret, reveal ...
Expressions of uncertainty	doubtful, inexact, suspicion, perhaps, possibly ...
Methodology	concept, theory, method ...

2. Turn the following informal expressions into formal ones.

Informal expressions	Formal expressions
I think ...	
Steve Jobs is a computer geek! point out ...	
To improve the air quality, we should reduce the use of private cars.	
Many people think that ...	
More younger generations celebrate the Western festivals. (nominalization)	

3. Give synonyms to the following phrasal verbs, which tend to be used in academic writing.

Phrasal verbs	Synonyms
ask for	
catch on	

Phrasal verbs	Synonyms
check up on	
find out	
set up	
cut down	
go up	
come up with	
look into	
go up and down	
bring up	
get rid of	
turn down	
make up for	

4. Please rewrite the following sentences in a formal style.

   a. That is a **perfect** idea.

   _____

   b. **There were more** foreign teachers in the university than the natives.

   _____

   c. You have to remember that the primary data needs to be recorded immediately.

   _____

Task D | Critical Thinking: Ways to lose weight

1. Work in groups. Prepare a conversation that you can present to the whole class. Make notes if necessary.
   1) Think about the question of the various ways to lose weight. Do you agree or disagree with the result in the above excerpt "How Might Exercise Affect Our Food Choices and Our Weight?"?
   2) How do you think of the experiment in the excerpt, which was published in November in *Medicine & Science in Sports & Exercise*?
   3) Compare with the other ways of losing weight, and tell us what is the best way for weight loss.

2. Present your conversation to other groups.

Notes

Glossary of Unit 6

Reading 1

obesity
n. a condition characterized by the excessive accumulation and storage of fat in the body
e. g. Obesity affects not just appearance, but disease processes as well.

malnourishment
n. faulty nutrition due to inadequate or unbalanced intake of nutrients or their impaired assimilation or utilization
synonym: malnutrition
e. g. Malnourishment is a condition that results from eating a diet in which nutrients are either not enough or are too much such that the diet causes health problems.

heighten
vt. to increase the amount or degree of; to make brighter or more intense; to bring out more strongly; to make more acute
e. g. The decision is likely to heighten tensions between the region and the rest of Spain.

compel
vt. to cause to do or occur by overwhelming pressure
e. g. Public opinion compelled her to sign the bill.

awareness
n. the quality or state of being aware; knowledge and understanding that something is happening or exists
e. g. They hope to raise awareness of endangered species, encouraging donations and attracting tourists to the region to support conservation efforts.

plunge
vt. to cause to enter a state or course of action usually suddenly, unexpectedly, or violently
e. g. ... plunged the nation into economic depression

integral
adj. essential to completeness
e. g. an integral part of the curriculum

unavoidable
adj. not avoidable
e. g. The accident was unavoidable.

dietary
adj. of or relating to a diet or to the rules of a diet
e. g. dietary guidelines

endemic
adj. belonging or native to a particular people or country; characteristic of or prevalent in a particular field, area, or environment
e. g. Africa, Asia and Latin America are regions where rabies is endemic.

nutritionist
n. a specialist in the study of nutrition
e. g. The team now has its own wax truck, nutritionist, physical therapist and sports psychologist.

nuisance
n. one that is annoying, unpleasant, or

obnoxious

e. g. My allergies are a nuisance in the springtime.

adolescent

n. a young person who is developing into an adult; one who is in the state of adolescence

adj. of, relating to, or being in adolescence; emotionally or intellectually immature

e. g. adolescent boys and girls

gravity

n. dignity or sobriety of bearing; a serious situation or problem

e. g. a person of gravity and learning

relentless

adj. showing or promising no abatement of severity, intensity, strength, or pace

e. g. a relentless campaign

idiot

n. a foolish or stupid person

e. g. ... Idiot that I am to wear my heart on my sleeve! ...

vulnerable

adj. capable of being physically or emotionally wounded; open to attack or damage; liable to increased penalties but entitled to increased bonuses after winning a game in contract bridge

e. g. This procedure has improved, but it is still vulnerable to criticism.

disorder

vt. to disturb the order of; to disturb the regular or normal functions of

n. lack of order; breach of the peace or public order; an abnormal physical or mental condition

e. g. a personality disorder

diabetes

n. any of various abnormal conditions characterized by the secretion and excretion of excessive amounts of urine

e. g. diabetes medicine

stroke

n. a sudden loss of consciousness resulting when the rupture or occlusion of a blood vessel leads to oxygen lack in the brain

e. g. Stroke, also known as cerebrovascular accident (CVA), cerebrovascular insult (CVI), or brain attack, is when poor blood flow to the brain results in cell death.

infectious

adj. producing or capable of producing infection; caused by or resulting from an infection with one or more pathogenic agents; spreading or capable of spreading rapidly to others

e. g. Her happiness was infectious.

breastfeed

vt. to feed (a baby) from a mother's breast; to breastfeed a baby

e. g. ... more women are breastfeeding than ever before ...

hectic

adj. characterized by activity, excitement, or confusion

e. g. the hectic days before the holidays

menace

n. a threat or the act of threatening; a show of intention to inflict harm; an annoying person

e. g. ... exploding in menaces and threats of vengeance ...

inculcate

vt. to teach and impress by frequent repetitions or admonitions

e. g. It also aims to inculcate values such as telling the truth or not stealing.

Reading 2

alter
v. to make different without changing into something else
e. g. an event that altered the course of history

compelling
adj. demanding attention; convincing
e. g. a compelling personality

novice
n. a person admitted to probationary membership in a religious community
e. g. The novices spend part of each day in prayer and meditation.

underscore
v. to draw a line under; to make evident
e. g. ... arrived early to underscore the importance of the occasion ...

complexity
n. something complex; the quality or state of being complex
e. g. the complexities of the murder trial

recruit
v. to fill up the number of ... with new members
e. g. recruit an army

inactive
adj. lacking activity; lying idle or unused; of a disease (quiescent)
e. g. Illness forced him to live an inactive life.

questionnaire
n. a set of questions for obtaining statistically useful or personal information from individuals
e. g. a survey made by the use of a questionnaire

binge
n. an act of excessive or compulsive consumption (as of food)
e. g. ... went on an eating binge ...

overeat
v. to eat to excess
e. g. Overeating is the excess food in relation to the energy that an organism expends (or expels via excretion), leading to weight gaining and often obesity. It may be regarded as an eating disorder.

alteration
n. the result of changing or altering something; the act or process of altering something
e. g. The dress needs alteration for a proper fit.

irresistible
adj. impossible to resist
e. g. The silver-bright sap is irresistible to the insects.

psychological
adj. of or relating to psychology; mental; directed toward the will or toward the mind specifically in its conative function
e. g. psychological warfare

instance
n. a step, stage, or situation viewed as part of a process or series of events
e. g. The donor prefers, in this instance, to remain anonymous.

trait
n. a distinguishing quality (as of personal character)
e. g. Curiosity is one of her notable traits.

susceptibility
n. the quality or state of being susceptible,

especially lack of ability to resist some extraneous agent (such as a pathogen or drug); sensitivity

e. g. <u>Susceptibility</u> has little to do with fitness.

overconsume

v. to consume too much of (something)

e. g. We're <u>overconsuming</u> processed foods, sugar, saturated fat and sodium.

dietitian

n. a specialist in dietetics

e. g. A <u>dietitian</u> alters their patient's nutrition based upon their medical condition and individual needs.

nudge

v. to push into action by pestering or annoying gently

e. g. Behavioral economists like to talk about <u>nudge</u> theory.

UK Government Criticized Over Food Security and Poverty

Academics Tim Lang, Terry Marsden and Erik Millstone have criticised the UK Government over "Neo-Victorian" levels of food poverty as well as failing to safeguard the country's food supply and security. In an open letter they have urged Prime Minister Boris Johnson to invest in adequate infrastructure to ensure food security for the future.

Food policy has been an embarrassing issue for the Conservative government, who performed a series of U-turns over the provision of free school meals for children after campaigns by the footballer Marcus Rashford. Rashford has called for an urgent review of food provisions for the poorest children in the country following his campaign.

"Food poverty is now in the neo-Victorian mode of relying on food banks, but they cannot keep up with rising demand," said Millstone, a professor at the University of Sussex. "Poor diet and poor health has undoubtedly contributed to the UK's appalling Covid death rate, particularly among families on low incomes, and this needs to be the catalyst for a major change."

The academics have said that not enough has been done in the UK, both with regard to Brexit and COVID-19, to prepare the country for potential crises.

Among their recommendations they say:

- Deploying resources from the closed hospitality sector to provide emergency food centers.
- Instructing government organizations to produce nutritional advice on foods consumers should be choosing to protect themselves against the threat of Covid-19.
- Creating an independent council to provide advice on the long-term direction for the UK agri-food system to improve food security.

UK food security in the spotlight

Professor Erik Millstone and Professor Tim Lang will be appearing at Food Matters Live in March to join a live webcast focused on food security in the UK. The fragility of the UK's food system was exposed at the height of the pandemic. Now as we move to a new era beyond BREXIT, reflecting on the learnings from the first three months, our panel of policy makers, industry leaders and academics will look at how the UK's food system must evolve in light of trade deals & tariffs, increases in food prices and the growing number of people facing food poverty.

The session is part of the Global Food Futures program at Food Matters Live that focuses on geopolitics, food security and sustainability across the world, and how the industry can help solve these challenges.

Posted: 16/02/21

Source: UK Government criticized over food security and poverty. (2021, February 16). *Food Matters*. Retrieved May 20, 2021, from https://www.foodmatters.co.uk/news/uk-government-criticised-over-food-security-andpoverty/.

Unit 7

Business and Job Hunting

Nowadays, the job market competition seems to be quite intense and fierce. As a college student, it is necessary for you to get to know current employment situation. In this unit, you will get to know gender inequalities in job market, and will get to know the first thing you are going to face when you apply for a job. You will learn the features of an editorial and an illustration essay, as well as how to express your idea by using appropriate verbs. You will also get to know some vocabulary to describe personalities, which might be helpful for introducing yourself when you are seeking for a job in the future.

By the end of this unit, you will be able to:	
SKILL	TASK
learn the features of an editorial	• Reading 1 • Task A
get to know metaphors	• Reading 1 • Task B
discover the metaphors in the context	• Reading 1 • Task B
learn verbs to introduce one's opinion	• Reading 1 • Task C
use the verbs to introduce opinions independently	• Reading 1 • Task C
compare the similarities and differences between cultures	• Reading 1 • Task D
learn the features of an illustration essay	• Reading 2 • Task A
learn the suffixes -ion and -ence	• Reading 2 • Task B
change the word into noun form by using the suffixes -ion and -ence	• Reading 2 • Task B
learn vocabulary related to personalities	• Reading 2 • Task C
describe the personality of one person	• Reading 2 • Task C
evaluate the effectiveness of a psychological test	• Reading 2 • Task D

READING & CRITICAL THINKING

Reading 1

Pre-reading activity

1. Reading 1 is an editorial about gender equality in the workplace from *The Economist*. Read the following material and get some knowledge about *The Economist*.

> **An Introduction to *The Economist***
>
> ➢ *The Economist* is an English-language weekly newspaper owned by the Economist Group and edited in offices in London. Continuous publication began under the founder James Wilson in September 1843.
>
> ➢ Although *The Economist* has a global emphasis and scope, about two-thirds of the 75 staff journalists are based in London.
>
> ➢ *The Economist* claims that it "is not a chronicle of economics". Rather, it aims "to take part in a severe contest between intelligence, which presses forward, and an unworthy, timid ignorance obstructing our progress".
>
> ➢ It takes an editorial stance of classical and economic liberalism which is supportive of free trade, globalisation, free immigration and cultural liberalism (such as supporting legal recognition for same-sex marriage).
>
> ➢ It targets highly educated readers and claims an audience containing many influential executives and policy-makers.
>
> Source: The economist. (2021, August 31). (n. d.). *Wikipedia*. Retrieved August 31, 2021, from https://en.jinzhao.wiki/wiki/The_Economist.

2. Here are some opinions with regard to the injustices faced by working women. Read them and think about the following questions:
   a. To what extent do you agree or disagree with the opinions listed here?
   b. What are the other gender stereotypes you have noticed in the daily life? Set some examples.

(1) **Talking at meetings**

Men who speak up are perceived as being in control, while women who speak up are seen as "pushy".

(2) **Eye contact**

If both of the male and the female are meeting or interviewing someone, that person will make eye contact with the male during 80 percent of the conversation. It sends a clear signal that the person sees the male (me) as more influential and important than my female colleague.

(3) **Language style**

Women tend to use more inclusive language when talking about their teams, goals and strategies, while men tend to use more competitive and forceful words.

(4) **Reporting grievances**

When a man brings up problems and conflicts at work, he's often seen as direct and honest—even courageous. When a woman raises the same grievances, she may be characterized as whiny or overly sensitive. Like other items on this list, this perception is fueled by gender stereotypes.

(5) **Interacting with colleagues**

Let's say there's an important engineering team made up of males. That team interacts regularly with a product development team that happens to have two leads—a man and a woman—both with similar jobs. The man regularly jokes with the engineering team and builds rapport. But when the woman does the same thing, she risks being characterized as a flirt. As a result, she spends less time with the engineers and doesn't build the same kind of rapport. Surely the male will be more successful getting their projects prioritized.

(6) **Ideas from men vs women**

Too often a woman will present an idea in a meeting only to have it dismissed or ignored. But when a male colleague restates essentially the same concept—possibly with greater confidence—the team decides it's a magnificent idea.

Source: Hiner, J. (2015, May 9). Everyday injustices for working women: The slights add up. *Cnet.com*. Retrieved August 31, 2021, from https://www.cnet.com/news/everyday-injustice-the-slights-add-up/.

A Woman's Work

¹ Women have made great strides in the employment market over the past 50 years. But many still feel that their progress is being obstructed and, to coincide with International Women's Day on March 8th, two new books by feminist writers tackle the issues.

² In "The Fix" Michelle King, director of inclusion at Netflix, a video-streaming giant, observes that women are constantly told they need to change themselves—be more assertive, work longer hours and so on. Instead, she argues, working practices should change to accommodate the needs of half the adult population. In "The Home Stretch" Sally Howard, a journalist, suggests that a big reason why women are held back is that even those who work full-time are still expected to do the bulk of the housework. To cite the book's lengthy but apposite subtitle, she makes a strong case "why it's time to come clean about who does the dishes".

³ Male managers may find these books an uncomfortable read, peppered with talk of the patriarchy and gender privilege. Sometimes, the authors go too far. Ms. Howard links the patriarchy with capitalism so often that one wonders whether she has ever seen a picture of the Soviet Union's all-male politburo.

⁴ But men do not need to forsake the capitalist system to appreciate the plight of female workers. They just need empathy. Are women in the workplace judged by the same standards as their male colleagues? Are they described with adjectives (strident or emotional, for example) that would not be applied to men with the same characteristics?

⁵ Despite recent progress, women still face a glass ceiling. A couple of stories in Ms. King's book illustrate the point. Sarah was an executive at a

multinational who worked late, underwent management training and enthusiastically received and acted on feedback. After many years of rejection, it seemed she was due for promotion to the next tier, which was 100% male. But at the key meeting a male executive said: "I don't know; she just doesn't fit. She has those glasses and she wears that clip in her hair." Not exactly "scientific management".

6 In the other tale Ms. King, on her first day in a new job, walked into a kitchen full of men. Her boss said, "Hey, Michelle, there are dishes in the sink and you are a woman, so, you know, wash them." His colleagues laughed. When she protested, she was told to learn to take a joke.

7 Bullying disguised as humour is still bullying. And women are expected to put up with it. They must also tolerate different dress standards. Boris Johnson, Britain's prime minister, often messes up his hair before public appearances to maintain his "lovable buffoon" image. Dominic Cummings, his adviser, dresses scruffily, which suits his persona as the "eccentric genius". It is hard to imagine any woman reaching position of political power while adopting a similar style.

8 Sometimes the excuse for the lack of female progress in certain professions is that women and men naturally choose to pursue different career paths. Yet those outcomes may simply be the result of formal or informal barriers against female success. At the end of the 19th century, when only 4%–5% of American doctors were women, some men no doubt put this down to a lack of aptitude. Many medical schools, perhaps sharing that preconception, did not admit female candidates; Harvard's began accepting women only after the second world war. In Britain women were not allowed to become practising lawyers until they were admitted to the Law Society in 1922.

9 In both professions the playing field was eventually levelled. The result in 2017 more women were admitted to American medical schools than men for the first time. By 2018 half of British solicitors were female.

10 Another common argument is that it makes sense for married people

to specialise, with the man taking on higher-paid employment and the woman doing more of the chores. It is equally dubious. One study, for instance, found that husbands who earn less than their wives do even less housework than those who earn more.

[11] Many of the arguments that women's lack of progress is down to aptitude or choice look like a convenient fiction for men, who do rather well out of the bargain. Women, who end up doing most of the chores as well as working long hours, get a raw deal. It is not them who need to change—it is the attitudes of men.

Source: A woman's work. (2020, March 11). (n. d.). *kekenet.com*. Retrieved May 11, 2020, from http://www.kekenet.com/menu/202003/606371.shtml.

Post-reading activity

Task A | Reading Comprehension Strategy: Features of an editorial

What is an editorial?

★ An editorial is an opinion piece written by the senior editorial staff or publisher of a newspaper, magazine, or any other written document. Editorials may be supposed to reflect the opinion of the periodical.

What is the structure of an editorial?

- Usually, an editorial is divided into three parts: beginning, body and conclusion.
- In the beginning part, the author tends to give the background information of a social phenomenon.
- In the body part, the author may give some further examples to show how serious the phenomenon is in the society, as well as give remarks/critiques after presenting examples.
- In the conclusion part, the author shows his/her attitude towards the phenomenon.

Discussion

Read the passage, and think about the following questions:

In the beginning part
1. What is the social phenomenon that the author wants to discuss?
2. What is the background information offered about the phenomenon?

Make some notes here to guide your discussion.	

In the body part
3. How many examples does the author give to talk about the phenomenon?
4. What kind of remarks does the author give with regard to each example?

Make some notes here to guide your discussion.	

In the conclusion part
5. What is the author's attitude towards the phenomenon?

Make some notes here to guide your discussion.	

Task B | Language Spotlight: Metaphors

What is a metaphor?

★ **A metaphor** is a word or phrase for one thing that is used to refer to another thing in order to show or suggest that they are similar. It is an object, activity, or idea that is used as a symbol of something else.

★ Metaphors are a form of figurative language, which refers to words or expressions that mean something different from their literal definition. Here are two examples:
  ◇ Love is a battlefield.
  ◇ Bob is a couch potato.

★ Metaphors can make your words come to life. Often, you can use a metaphor to make your subject more relatable to the reader or to make a complex thought easier to understand.

Source: Underwood, A. E. M. (2021). Metaphors. *Grammarly Blog*. Retrieved August 31, 2021, from https://www.grammarly.com/blog/metaphor.

Discussion

Please appreciate the following famous metaphors, and collect relevant background information if necessary and guess the meaning.

1. America has tossed its cap over the wall of space. —John F. Kennedy
2. Chaos is a friend of mine. —Bob Dylan
3. A good conscience is a continual Christmas. —Benjamin Franklin

Make some notes here to guide your discussion.	

Exercises

Discover the metaphors in Reading 1:

1. List all of them (write down the number of the paragraph and the whole sentence) in the following table:

The number of the paragraph	The sentence in which the metaphor lies
e. g. Paragraph 4	e. g. Sentence 1: But men do not need to forsake the capitalist system to appreciate the plight of female workers.

2. Discuss with your partners and appreciate the implied meaning of each sentence.

Make some notes here to guide your discussion.	

Task C | Vocabulary Practice: Verbs used to introduce one's opinion

When we read news or editorials, we can find ideas from the experts in the examples or opinions of the author.
Here are some verbs that we can use to indicate our ideas/opinions:
- ★ say/present/argue/show/feel ...
- ★ suggest/indicate/illustrate ...
- ★ talk about/put forward/point out ...

Exercise

Discover the verbs used to introduce the opinions in Reading 1 and list all of them by writing down the number of the paragraph and the whole sentence in the following table:

The number of the paragraph	The sentence
e. g. Paragraph 1 ……	e. g. Sentence 2: But many still feel that their progress is being obstructed and, to coincide with International Women's Day on March 8th, two new books by feminist writers tackle the issues.

Task D | Critical Thinking: Similarities and differences between cultures

Here is a piece of news discussing the status of working women in China:

Expert: China's Working Women Still Face Problems

Although China has a higher proportion of working women than other Asia-Pacific countries, it still faces problems in women's employment, according to an expert.

Lynn Myers, project official of the UN Women China Office, said at a conference entitled International Development and Regional Women Progress—Women's Development Roundtable, that some 71 percent of Chinese women are employed, which is much higher than in member countries of the International Organization for Economic Cooperation and Development or other Asia-Pacific countries.

According to the information provided by the All-China Women's Federation, China has more than 30 million women entrepreneurs, of whom 41 percent are self-employed and private entrepreneurs, accounting for 25 percent of all entrepreneurs in the country, Myers said.

The Women's Development Roundtable was held on May 24 in Xi'an, the capital of Shaanxi Province, aiming to further promote gender equality in China.

However, the project official said, Chinese women still face many obstacles such as a higher proportion of women in low-paying sectors, lack of channels to access funds and assets, an increasing gap in gender wages and a high risk of poverty in old age caused by unequal retirement policies.

In order to encourage equal employment opportunities and resources for women, Myers said, the UN Women China Office has established cooperative relations with many Chinese companies and top universities on a number of projects.

Mu Hong, director of the international department of the All-China Women's Federation, said the strategic concept of the Silk Road economic belt development proposed by President Xi Jinping provides new opportunities for women in the countries along the Silk Road through China, Central Asia and Europe.

Mu said her federation will work with women's organizations in other countries and international women's organizations to further promote the continuous development of gender equality.

Source: Lu, H. Y. & Ma, L. (2014, May 27). China's working women still face problems. *Chinadaily*. Retrieved September 8, 2021, from http://www.chinadaily.com.cn/china/2014-05/27/content_17543770.htm.

Discussion

Compare the status of working women in Britain and in China, and discuss the following questions. You can take notes in the table.
1. What are the similarities of the status between British working women and Chinese working women?
2. What are the differences of the status between British working women and Chinese working women?
3. What are the reasons for working women facing the difficulties?
4. Do you have any suggestions to solve the problem faced by working women nowadays?

Notes
Question 1
Question 2
Question 3
Question 4

Reading 2
Companies Are Relying More and More on Psychometric Tests

¹ Here is a test. Assign a score of 1 to 5, where 1 is "strongly agree" and 5 is strongly disagree, to the following statement: "I really care about my work." If you have answered that kind of question before, you have probably applied for a job at a large company. Psychometric tests, as they are called, have become increasingly popular.

² Eager job-seekers may think the answers to these questions are glaringly obvious. For any statement, give a response that creates a portrait of a diligent, collaborative worker. Of course, applicants care about their work, love collaborating with other people and pay careful attention to detail. But the people who set the tests know that candidates will respond in this way. So questions are rephrased in many different ways to check that applicants are consistent and make it difficult for them to remember what they have already said.

³ Aptitude tests are not a new idea. Intelligence tests have been around for a century and were popular with government departments. Charles Johnson, who has been involved in psychometric testing for 40 years and was responsible for constructing the tests used to recruit British civil servants says the second world war had a big impact. The British were impressed with the efficiency of German army officers and learned they had been selected with the help of intelligence tests. This led the British to create the War Office Selection Board. Alongside verbal and non-verbal reasoning, it challenged candidates with word-association exercises and being made to lead group discussions.

⁴ For high-skilled jobs, these tests are useful. However, Mr. Johnson says there is a risk with using such tests to recruit workers for low-skilled jobs. If you select people who pass sophisticated cognitive tests, they will learn the job quickly but will then get bored and leave.

⁵ Psychometric tests became more popular from the 1970s onwards and are now seen as a useful way of sorting through the many candidates who apply for the jobs offered by big companies. "It is a laborious task to sort through thousands of written applications," says Julia Knight, another occupational psychologist. "As well as being time consuming, it is not very effective and subject to bias."

⁶ Questions in such tests may ask a candidate to describe their behaviour in hypothetical situations: dealing with an angry customer, for example. The suggested answers may all be plausible (apologise profusely, fetch a manager and so on), so there is no obviously "right" answer. Nevertheless the aim is to build a profile of the candidate to see if they have the right character traits for the job.

⁷ People are generally judged on the basis of five characteristics with the acronym OCEAN for openness, conscientiousness, extroversion (or introversion), agreeableness and neuroticism. The ideal characteristics can be surprising: it turns out that introverts are the best train drivers as they seem to pay more attention to details such as safety procedures and can cope with spending long periods of their time on their own.

⁸ Extroverts do not make the best call centre employees because they can spend so much time chatting to customers that they don't get much done. The most useful trait among such workers, according to Steve Fletcher, an occupational psychologist, is assertiveness; this enables them to deal with more calls.

⁹ These tests are used to assess senior managers, as well as new hires. Along with OCEAN—characteristics, testers are also looking for what is known as the "dark triad"—psychopathy, narcissism and Machiavellianism.

Factors that can make people successful as junior managers may limit their ascent. Candidates who are good with detail turn out to be obsessive micromanagers; people who flourish in sales may have an excessive need to be the centre of attention.

[10] A large majority of big companies use these tests but they are hardly perfect. Paul Flowers, the former head of Coop Bank, a British lender, passed his psychometric tests with flying colours, according to testimony at a parliamentary inquiry. But he was later ousted in a sex-and-drugs scandal that led him to be dubbed "the crystal Methodist". Mr. Johnson says the tests can be useful, but only in conjunction with aptitude tests and structured interviews.

[11] That probably won't save job candidates from having to take these tests in future, because they win now down the list. But at least they beat the old-fashioned method: drop half the application in the bin and pick from the other half.

Source: Companies are relying more and more on psychometric tests. (2020, November 13). (n. d.). *kekenet. com.* Retrieved December 13, 2020, from http://www.kekenet.com/menu/202011/620638.shtml.

Task A | Reading Comprehension Strategy: Features of the illustration essay

What is an illustration essay?

★ An ***illustration essay*** is a form of writing which encloses examples to express an idea.

★ This type of essay requires you to provide specific details or patterns to clarify or justify the point you made.

★ Its purpose is to fully explain a notion, thought, situation, or concept. In other words, it illustrates or demonstrates an idea or something related to the topic through the use of examples.

Features of an illustration essay

★ It includes an introduction which states the thesis, a body which provides examples to prove the thesis, and a conclusion which restates the thesis.

★ It usually uses sayings, proverbs, phrases, analogies, or words that will be easily understood to hook readers.

★ A good illustrative essay starts with an interesting topic, a well-written introduction to grab the audience's attention, a body with very descriptive examples and a conclusion that summarizes the main points and has a solution to a problem.

Source: How to write an illustration essay. (2021). (n.d.). *Solid Essay*. Retrieved May 12, 2021, from https://www.solidessay.com/our-services/how-to-write-an-illustration-essay.

Discussion

Look at Reading 2, and think about the following questions:
1. What is the idea the author presents?
2. What are the examples the author uses to demonstrate the idea?
3. What is the conclusion the author makes?

Make some notes here to guide your discussion.	

Task B | Language Spotlight: Noun suffixes -ion & -ence

-ion It is added to some verbs in order to form nouns. Nouns formed in this way often refer to a state or process.

-ence It is added to adjectives/verbs to form nouns referring to states, qualities, attitudes, or behaviour.

Exercises

1. Change the verb into the noun form by adding the suffix -ion.

a. decide	
b. expand	
c. act	
d. connect	
e. compete	
f. hesitate	
g. attract	
h. imagine	

2. Change the adjective into the noun form by adding the suffix -ence.

a. absent	
b. different	
c. depend	
d. exist	
e. persistent	
f. consistent	
g. consequent	
h. emergent	

Discussion

Circle the words with the suffixes **-ion** or **-ence** in Reading 2, and guess the verb/adjective form of the noun words.

Task C | Vocabulary Practice: Words to describe personalities

Exercises

1. Match the adjectives describing personalities in Column A with the types of personalities in Column B.

Column A	Column B
humorous	extrovert
steady	introvert
independent	pessimist
active	optimist
vivacious	
adventurous	
temperate	
energetic	
obedient	
shy	
outspoken	

2. Find words to describe personalities in Reading 2 and list them here.

Words to describe personalities

3. Draw a picture or find a photo of a person, and describe him/her by using the words linked to personalities in Reading 2. You can take notes in the table.

Notes

Task D | Critical Thinking: The effectiveness of a psychological test/psychometric test

Discussion

Think about the following questions and discuss with your partners.
1. Have you ever done any kind of psychological test/psychometric test before?
2. What do you think of the effectiveness of the test?
3. What do you think of the idea presented in Reading 2 that many companies prefer using psychometric test? What are the advantages and disadvantages of this idea?

Make some notes here to guide your discussion.	

Glossary of Unit 7

Reading 1

stride
n. an improvement in the way sth. is developing
e. g. We're making great strides in the search for a cure.

obstruct
v. to prevent sb./sth. from doing sth. or making progress, especially when this is done deliberately
e. g. They were charged with obstructing the police in the course of their duty.

coincide
v. to happen at the same time
e. g. The exhibition coincides with the 50th anniversary of his death.

tackle
v. to make a determined effort to deal with a difficult problem or situation
e. g. The government is determined to tackle inflation.

observe
v. (formal) to make a remark
e. g. She observed that it was getting late.

assertive
adj. expressing opinions or desires strongly and with confidence, so that people take notice
e. g. You should try and be more assertive.

bulk
n. the main part of sth.; most of sth.
e. g. The bulk of the population lives in cities.

apposite
adj. (formal) very appropriate for a particular situation or in relation to sth.
e. g. Recent events have made his central theme even more apposite.

patriarchy
n. a society, system or country that is ruled or controlled by men
e. g. The main cause of women's and children's oppression is patriarchy.

privilege
n. a special right or advantage that a particular person or group of people has
e. g. Education should be a universal right and not a privilege.

capitalism
n. an economic system in which a country's businesses and industry are controlled and run for profit by private owners rather than by the government
e. g. ... the two fundamentally opposed social systems, capitalism and socialism.

forsake
v. to stop doing sth., using sth., or having sth.
e. g. She forsook the glamour of the city and went to live in the wilds of Scotland.

plight
n. a difficult and sad situation
e. g. The African elephant is in a desperate plight.

multinational

adj. existing in or involving many countries

e.g. A multinational force is being sent to the trouble spot.

executive

n. a person who has an important job as a manager of a company or an organization

e.g. an advertising executive.

empathy

n. the ability to understand another person's feelings, experience, etc.

e.g. empathy for other people's situations

illustrate

v. to make the meaning of sth. clearer by using examples, pictures, etc.

e.g. To illustrate my point, let me tell you a little story.

rejection

n. to refuse sth.

e.g. These feelings of rejection and hurt remain.

protest

v. to say or do sth. to show that you disagree with or disapprove of sth., especially publicly

e.g. Students took to the streets to protest against the decision.

eccentric

adj. considered by other people to be strange or unusual

e.g. He is an eccentric character who likes wearing a beret and dark glasses.

barrier

n. a problem, rule or situation that prevents sb. from doing sth., or that makes sth. impossible

e.g. Lack of confidence is a psychological barrier to success.

aptitude

n. natural ability or skill at doing sth.

e.g. His aptitude for dealing with children got him the job.

preconception

n. an idea or opinion that is formed before you have enough information or experience

e.g. This is a book that will challenge your preconceptions about rural life.

level

v. to make sth. equal or similar

e.g. Davies levelled the score at 2 all.

solicitor

n. (BrE) a lawyer who prepares legal documents, for example, for the sale of land or buildings, advises people on legal matters, and can speak for them in some courts of law

e.g. He has always been the family solicitor.

dubious

adj. not certain and slightly suspicious about sth.; not knowing whether sth. is good or bad

e.g. I was rather dubious about the whole idea.

hold back

(to hold sb. or sth. back) to prevent sb. from doing sth., or to prevent sth. from happening

e.g. Stagnation in home sales is holding back economic recovery.

come clean (about)

to make sth. clear

e.g. I think you have to come clean.

pepper sth. with sth.

to include large numbers of sth. in sth.

e.g. He peppered his speech with jokes.

prime minister

the main minister and leader of the government in some countries

e. g. The Prime Minister is visiting Japan at the moment.

end up

to find yourself in a place or situation that you did not intend or expect to be in

e. g. I ended up doing all the work myself.

raw deal

unequal treatment

e. g. I think women have a raw deal.

job-seeker

n. an unemployed person who is trying to get a job

e. g. This is good advice for any job-seeker, but more so with the older ones.

glaringly

adv. very easily seen

e. g. The hardest thing to explain is the glaringly evident which everybody had decided not to see.

portrait

n. a detailed description of sb./sth.

e. g. I love this novel because it draws a vivid portrait of country lifestyle in Britain.

diligent

adj. (formal) showing care and effort in your work or duties

e. g. He is both wise and diligent, so he makes good in everything.

collaborative

adj. (formal) involving, or done by, several people or groups of people working together

e. g. It is important to develop a collaborative team culture.

rephrase

v. to say or write sth. using different words in order to make the meaning clearer

e. g. Can you please rephrase your question?

recruit

v. to find new people to join a company, an organization, the armed forces, etc.

e. g. They recruited several new members to the club.

verbal

adj. relating to words

e. g. The job applicant must have good verbal skills.

reasoning

n. the process of thinking about things in a logical way; opinions and ideas that are based on logical thinking

e. g. What is the reasoning behind this decision?

association

n. an idea or a memory that is suggested by sb./sth.; a mental connection between ideas

e. g. The seaside had all sorts of pleasant associations with childhood holidays for me.

sophisticated

adj. clever and complicated in the way that it works or is presented

e. g. Medical techniques are becoming more sophisticated all the time.

cognitive

adj. connected with mental processes of understanding

e. g. What people wear can affect their cognitive performance.

onwards

adv. continuing from a particular time

e.g. They lived there from the 1980s onwards.

laborious

adj. taking a lot of time and effort

e.g. Checking all the information will be slow and laborious.

occupational

adj. connected with a person's job or profession

e.g. I have an occupational pension.

bias

n. a strong feeling in favour of or against one group of people, or one side in an argument, often not based on fair judgement

e.g. Employers must consider all candidates impartially and without bias.

hypothetical

adj. based on situations or ideas which are possible and imagined rather than real and true

e.g. I wasn't asking about anybody in particular—it was just a hypothetical question.

plausible

adj. reasonable and likely to be true

e.g. The only plausible explanation is that he forgot.

profile

n. a description of sb./sth. that gives useful information

e.g. We first build up a detailed profile of our customers and their requirements.

conscientiousness

n. the condition or quality of taking care to do things carefully and correctly

e.g. What really counts in the world is conscientiousness.

extroversion

n. the act, state, or habit of being predominantly concerned with and obtaining gratification from what is outside the self

e.g. Then I was changed from introversion to extroversion.

trait

n. a particular quality in your personality

e.g. Honesty proves to be a very important trait of a person.

assertiveness

n. the quality of expressing opinions or desires strongly and with confidence, so that people take notice

e.g. Assertiveness is a learned skill.

narcissism

n. (formal, disapproving) the habit of admiring yourself too much, especially your appearance

e.g. Narcissism and creativity seem to go hand in hand.

ascent

n. (formal) the process of moving forward to a better position or of making progress

e.g. man's ascent to civilization

obsessive

adj. thinking too much about one particular person or thing, in a way that is not normal

e.g. He's becoming more and more obsessive about punctuality.

flourish

v. to achieve success

e.g. Business flourished and within six months they were earning 18,000 roubles a day.

excessive

adj. greater than what seems reasonable or

appropriate

e. g. They complained about the excessive noise coming from the upstairs flat.

scandal

n. behaviour or an event that people think is morally or legally wrong and causes public feelings of shock or anger

e. g. There has been no hint of scandal during his time in office.

dub

v. to give sb./sth. a particular name, often in a humorous or critical way

e. g. The Belgian actor Jean Claude Van Damme has been dubbed "Muscles from Brussels".

winnow

v. If you winnow a group of things or people, you reduce its size by separating the ones that are useful or relevant from the ones that are not.

e. g. Administration officials have winnowed the list of candidates to three.

old-fashioned

adj. not modern; no longer fashionable

e. g. By the second or third generation, such old-fashioned attitudes are generally forgotten.

civil servant

n. a person who works for the local, state, or federal government in the United States, or in the civil service in Britain and some other countries

e. g. He is a civil servant, with a bachelor's degree.

be subject to

likely to be affected by sth., especially sth. bad

e. g. Flights are subject to delay because of the fog.

cope with

to deal successfully with sth. difficult

e. g. He wasn't able to cope with the stresses and strains of the job.

on one's own

alone; without anyone else

e. g. She lives on her own.

in conjunction with

(formal) together with

e. g. The police are working in conjunction with tax officers on the investigation.

Some Unfortunate Mismatches in Young People's Job Preferences and Prospects

The world of work is changing. Are people ready for the new job outlook? A survey of 15-year-olds across 41 countries by the OECD, a club of mostly rich countries found that teenagers may have unrealistic expectations about the kind of work that will be available.

Four of the five most popular choices were traditional professional roles doctors, teachers, business managers and lawyers. Teenagers clustered around the most popular jobs, with the top ten being chosen by 47% of boys and 53% of girls. Those shares were significantly higher than when the survey was conducted back in 2000.

The rationale for this selection was partly down to wishful thinking on the part of those surveyed (designers, actors and musical performers were three of the top 15 jobs). Youth must be allowed a bit of hope. When Bartleby was a teenager, his ambitions were to play cricket for England and become prime minister; neither ambition was achieved (a lucky escape for the country on both counts).

Furthermore, teenagers can hardly be expected to have an in-depth knowledge of the minutiae of labour-market trends. They will have encountered doctors and teachers in their daily lives. Other popular professions, such as lawyers and police officers, will be familiar from films and social media. But many people end up in jobs they would not have heard of in their school years. You settle for what is available.

The OECD points out that some of the fastest-growing occupations are rarely mentioned by young people. But surely the surprise is not that "user support technician" is ranked only the 158th out of 543 professions and "computer user support specialist" appears in the 229th place. Rather, it is astonishing that young people know that such jobs exist at all.

At least teenagers who want to tackle climate change, as many profess to, are in luck. America's Bureau of Labour Statistics (bls) predicts that the two fastest-growing occupations over the next few years will be solar-photo-installers and wind-turbine technicians.

Some parts of the OECD survey are disturbing. Even though top performers in maths or science are evenly matched among males and females, a gender gap persists in terms of aspiration. More boys than girls expect to work in science or engineering—average gap across the OECD is more than ten percentage points. The problem continues in higher education; with the exception of biological and biomedical sciences, degrees in stem subjects (science, technology, engineering and maths) are male-dominated. In America women earn just 35.5% of undergraduate stem degrees and 33.7% of PHDs.

Things are even worse in technology. In Britain only one in five computer-science university students is a woman—a big problem at time when the World Economic Forum predicts that technology will create more than a quarter of all jobs in newly emerging professions. But women are underrepresented in some important fields of technology; they have only 12% of jobs in cloud computing, for example. Something about the tech industry puts off female applicants.

Source: Some unfortunate mismatches in young people's job preferences and prospects. (2020, February 22). (n.d.). *kekenet.com*. Retrieved May 22, 2020, from http://xiu.kekenet.com/play/605425.

Environmental Protection

Plastic is incredibly useful. From medical instruments and computers to lightweight, unbreakable containers, plastic seems to be in just about everything we use and has clearly made all of our lives easier. However, it's not easy to recycle it effectively and takes a very long time to break down naturally. Therefore, it builds up and causes terrible pollution, which has become one of the most pressing environmental issues. In this unit, you will examine some key facts about plastic pollution. You will learn that recycling and responsible disposal are the best measures for reducing and controlling plastic trash. You will look at features that are typical in an academic context, such as words with multiple meanings, word formation, discourse signals, text patterns, etc., and will practice using them appropriately.

By the end of this unit, you will be able to:	
SKILL	TASK
identify pros and cons	• Reading 1 • Task A
identify homonyms	• Reading 1 • Task B
recognize and practice affixes accurately	• Reading 1 • Task C
examine the meaning of new words according to the context	• Reading 1 • Task C
learn to evaluate the consequences of using plastic production	• Reading 1 • Task D
find out possible measures individuals can take in their daily life to protect the environment	• Reading 1 • Task D
learn to organize information by creating a concept map	• Reading 2 • Task A
learn to identify cause and effect signal words	• Reading 2 • Task B
practice linking ideas by using cause and effect signal words	• Reading 2 • Task B
understand words with multiple meanings	• Reading 2 • Task C
learn to reflect on the content of the text	• Reading 2 • Tasks D

Reading 1

Pre-reading activity

The following description is about plastic pollution in the ocean and its effect on our food chain, but some information is missing. With a partner, fill in the blanks using the statistics shown below.

672   35%   18   86%   44%   43%   one million   50   267   100,000

In the ocean, plastic debris injures and kills ocean wildlife.
In all, __1__ marine species are affected by plastic refuse, including __2__ of all sea turtle species, __3__ of all seabird species, and __4__ of all marine mammal species. Plastic bags and other plastic debris can account for the deaths of __5__ birds, more than __6__ whales, seals, and turtles, and countless fish worldwide every year. In one case, a turtle only __7__ inches long had over __8__ plastic items in its stomach.

Plastic also has a significant impact on our own food chain.
In 2008, researchers on a Pacific Gyre voyage began finding that fish are ingesting plastic fragments and debris. Of the __9__ fish caught during that voyage, __10__ had ingested plastic pieces. In the environment, toxins tend to accumulate in the food chain. The higher up the food chain toxins enter, the higher the concentration of toxins. We are just one step up on the food chain from when the toxins enter it: fish eat plastic; people eat fish.

A World of Plastic Pollution

¹ How many plastic products do you use in your everyday life? Plastic is everywhere—from the tube your toothpaste comes in to the chair you sit on at school. It is an important part of electronic items such as toys, computers, and cell phones. Sometimes, plastic is an unseen part of our environment. For example, it is used for pipes in houses, essential parts in cars, and even in airplanes and rockets. It is resistant to harmful substances, good for insulation, and exceptionally versatile.

² Plastic is a manufactured material, made by humans. It is flexible and lightweight but also very strong. Plastic is more able to stand wear than other materials, such as wood, metal, paper. However, although plastic is a long-lasting material, it is often used in disposable products such as drink bottles, grocery bags, utensils, pens, and diapers.

Why people use plastic

³ People use plastic for a number of reasons:
  a) Plastic is very strong, and chemicals do not wear it away quickly. It provides non-breakable packages for dangerous liquids. Liquid leaning products are also packaged in plastic for safety.
  b) Plastic insulates against heat and electricity. Electrical appliances, leads, outlets, and wiring are usually made or covered with plastic. Plastic pot and pan handles protect against burning heat. Plastic is also used in the foam core of fridges and freezers, in insulated cups, coolers, and microwave cookware.
  c) Plastic is very light. Compared to stone, concrete, steel, copper, or aluminum, all plastics are lightweight.
  d) Plastic is versatile. It can be processed into very thin fibers or molded into large car parts such as dashboards and bumpers. It can be foamed into polystyrene or mixed with liquids to become adhesives or paints.
  e) Plastic comes in a countless range of types and colors. It can be made to mimic fabrics such as cotton, silk, and wool fibers; it feels like stone such as porcelain and marble or looks like metals such as aluminum and zinc. Plastics also come as clear sheets and flexible film.

Spotlight on plastic bags

4   Plastic grocery store bags are among the most common shopping items on Earth. Their light weight, low cost, and water resistance make them very convenient for carrying things, from groceries to clothing. It is hard to imagine life without them. They weigh just a few grams and are so thin that they might seem harmless. But the sheer numbers are amazing.

5   Each year, across the world, some 500 billion plastic bags are used, ranging from large garbage bags to thick shopping totes to flimsy grocery bags. Only a tiny fraction of them are recycled, and most are just thrown away. That is when the problems start. The world is choking on carelessly discarded plastic bags.

Fantastic plastic

6   Plastic has become an important and useful part of our world. But the strength and durability of plastic has a flip side. The world now finds itself polluted with disposable plastics that will not go away. They do not decompose, or break down, as fast as wood or paper. And when they do start to break down, they are harmful to the environment.

7   For these reasons and others, plastics are convenient and helpful. But, as people have realized, plastic has become controversial. Plastic increasingly threatens the environment as pollution on land and in the ocean.

No day in the sun with plastic

8   It may not seem as significant as the damage to the environment and human health, but people also suffer when shorelines, bays, beaches, and rivers are overrun with floating plastic pollution. If plastic garbage accumulates in those areas, how can people swim or enjoy the shoreline? Seaside towns suffer economically because they must spend money paying workers to dispose of the garbage. They may also lose out financially if tourists stop visiting their towns because of the pollution.

9   In one example, Jamaica spent around $294,000 cleaning up Kingston

Harbor in the wake of a tropical storm that caused plastic bottles to float and accumulate in large numbers. In towns where this happens frequently, daily garbage collection, or worse, piled-up bottles and plastics, mean trouble. Fewer tourists would come, damaging the local economy and disrupting people's lives.

10   In developing countries, if bays are choked with bottles and plastic refuse, the problem is not only a potential impact on tourism. The problem is the effect it has on local people's use of water for life and work. People can not freely come and go from docks, or anchor their boats, when bays are clogged. For towns with fishing industries, the ability to fish is restricted.

A recent realization

11   By the 1980s, there was so much visible plastic pollution that it was impossible to ignore. Plastic bottles littered beaches, plastic bags fluttered from tree branches, and disposable diapers polluted canals and rivers. Plastic was piling up so high because it does not biodegrade, or break down into the environment, very easily. People were throwing more and more disposable products away. This meant that landfill sites were filling up with items that may take up to a thousand years to decompose. All of those trillions of plastic bags, styrofoam cups, bottles, and plastic utensils will remain in landfills for a very long time. Suddenly, "disposable" did not seem so convenient any more.

12   Another cause for concern was the effect plastic pollution was having on wildlife. On land and in the ocean, plastic threatens to poison animals. In turn, this affects our food supply. In fact, most people support the idea of protecting the environment and wildlife. However, for some people, the harm caused by plastic pollution is not enough to outweigh the benefits to human safety and convenience that plastic provides. Many people do not believe that the effort and cost involved in protecting the environment is worth the inconvenience of limiting the use of plastic.

13   Fortunately, researchers have been examining these problems of plastic pollution and ways that plastic pollution might be fought, through people

Kingston educating themselves about the problem and, then, taking action. However, does the planet have enough time to wait for the solution? In the future, the whole world could be even more choked with plastic items than it is now! Due to the amount of plastic pollution already taking place, societies all around the world realize that they need to think about what to do with it. They also need to think about how to stop adding to the problem.

Adapted from: Knight, G. (2012). *Plastic Pollution*. Chicago: Heinemann-Raintree.

Post-reading activity

Task A | Reading Comprehension Strategy: Identifying pros and cons

1. Read the following passage and discuss these questions with a partner.
   1) What plastic products do you use in your everyday life?
   2) What good features do plastic bags have?
   3) What impact does plastic garbage have on seaside towns?

Identifying Pros and Cons

A writer may discuss both sides of an argument or an issue. Understanding arguments for an issue (*the pros*) and the reasons against it (*the cons*) can help you evaluate the author's claims and determine your position on the issue.

2. Look back at Reading 1. Complete the chart with the pros and cons of plastic items.

Pros of plastic items	Cons of plastic items
1.	1.
2.	2.
3.	3.
4.	4.
5.	5.
...	...

Task B | Language Spotlight: Identifying homonyms

When you read, you will often come across homonyms—words that have the same spelling and pronunciation, but have different meanings. Knowing the different possible meanings will improve your overall comprehension. You can usually tell the correct definition of a word by identifying its part of speech and by using the context (the words around it). For example,

high (*adv.*) at or to a position or level that is a long way up from the ground or from the bottom:
Plastic was piling up so **high** because it does not biodegrade, or break down into the environment, very easily.

high (*adj.*) greater or better than normal in quantity or quality, size or degree:
The daily case counts in some countries are still **high**.

With a partner, identify the meaning of the underlined words in the following pairs of sentences. You can use the context or a dictionary to help. Then complete the chart below.
 (1) a. Plastic is more able to stand wear than other materials, such as wood, metal, paper.
   b. Plastic is very strong, and chemicals do not wear it away quickly.
 (2) a. It provides non-breakable packages for dangerous liquids.

b. Liquid leaning products are also <u>packaged</u> in plastic for safety.
（3）a. Plastic is also used in the <u>foam</u> core of fridges and freezers, in insulated cups, coolers, and microwave cookware.
   b. It can be <u>foamed</u> into polystyrene or mixed with liquids to become adhesives or paints.
（4）a. Plastic pot and pan <u>handles</u> protect against burning heat.
   b. The government will have to be very careful in <u>handling</u> this issue.
（5）a. For towns with fishing industries, the ability to <u>fish</u> is restricted.
   b. There are many endangered species of <u>fish</u> in the world.
（6）a. In developing countries, if bays are choked with bottles and plastic <u>refuse</u>, the problem is not only a potential impact on tourism.
   b. The team leader <u>refuses</u> to acknowledge that there is a problem.

Words	Parts of speech	Meaning
wear	a.	a.
	b.	b.
package	a.	a.
	b.	b.
foam	a.	a.
	b.	b.
handle	a.	a.
	b.	b.
fish	a.	a.
	b.	b.
refuse	a.	a.
	b.	b.

Task C | Vocabulary Practice: Affixes

Affixes are word parts that are added to a word's base form to modify its meaning or to create a new word. Understanding the meaning of certain affixes can help you guess the meaning of unfamiliar vocabulary as you read. There are two types of affix: **prefixes** (at the beginning of a word) and **suffixes** (at the end of a word).

1. Read the information in the chart below.

Affix	Quality	Usual meaning
un-	privative prefix	not
non-	privative prefix	not
de-	verb prefix	remove from
over-	adjective/noun/verb prefix	to an excessive degree
-ant	adjective suffix	performing (a specified action) or being (in a specified condition)
-ance	noun suffix	instance of a quality or state
-able	adjective suffix	capable of, fit for, or worthy of

2. Look back at Reading 1. Find and write words that contain each prefix or suffix below.

   1) un- _____
   2) non- _____
   3) de- _____
   4) over- _____
   5) -ant _____
   6) -ance _____
   7) -able _____

3. With a partner, try to match the vocabulary in the columns to their meanings according to the context of the passage.

Word	Meaning
1. versatile (adj.)	a. to get rid of sth. that you no longer want or need
2. lightweight (adj.)	b. existing or continuing for a long time
3. long-lasting (adj.)	c. used to emphasize the size, degree or amount of sth.
4. insulate (v.)	d. to make it difficult for sth. to continue in the normal way
5. mimic (v.)	e. having many uses or applications
6. sheer (adj.)	f. to be made to look like sth. else
7. flimsy (adj.)	g. to separate from conducting bodies by means of nonconductors so as to prevent transfer of electricity, heat, or sound
8. choke (v.)	h. to gradually increase in number or quantity over a period of time
9. discard (v.)	i. to change back to a harmless natural state by the action of bacteria

(continuous)

Word	Meaning
10. accumulate (v.)	j. having less than average weight
11. disrupt (v.)	k. to block or fill a passage, space, etc. so that movement is difficult
12. biodegrade (v.)	l. thin and easily torn

Task D | Critical Thinking: Evaluating the content of a text

Discussion

Work in groups and discuss the questions. Give reasons to support your views.

1. The writer says, "... for some people, the harm caused by plastic pollution is not enough to outweigh the benefits to human safety and convenience that plastic provides. Many people do not believe that the effort and cost involved in protecting the environment is worth the inconvenience of limiting the use of plastic." Do you agree with these statements? Do you think the convenience and low cost of plastics outweigh the effect it has on the environment?

2. To reduce plastic production, individuals must consider changing their habits or routines. This is easier said than done, but some possible measures could still be taken. Make a list of things you can do in your daily life to cut down on the use of plastic and help protect the environment.

Note down your ideas below.

Reading 2

Dangers from E-waste

¹ E-waste is discarded electronic items such as computers, TVs, cell phones, and DVD players. People in developed countries eventually get rid of their old electronic products and buy new ones. Plastic is used in all of these items, usually as casing. But what to do with discarded electronics, the disposal of e-waste, is becoming a huge problem.

High-tech refuse

² In the United States, probably more than 70 percent of discarded computers, monitors, and TVs eventually end up in landfill sites, although a growing number of laws prohibit the dumping of e-waste due to the fact that it may leak toxins such as lead, mercury, and arsenic into the ground. The rest may go to recycling centers, or get sent overseas as part of well-meaning assistance programs. However, sending electronic equipment overseas as part of assistance programs raises issues of its own.

Africa

³ When shipping containers of secondhand computers first began arriving in Ghana in the mid-2000s, the intention was to help close the digital divide with developed countries. But these donations from Western aid organizations and Ghanaian authorities had unexpected consequences. It is illegal to export scrap computers. However, dishonest exporters of old computers in the West learned to label scrap computers as "donations" and send them overseas.

⁴ Today, perhaps as many as 50 percent of computer shipments overseas are scrap. To dispose of the computers, people burn them in order to salvage the metals, such as copper, contained inside the plastic casing. This is sometimes called the new mining industry.

5   Burning the plastic computer cases releases harmful toxins into the air. The workers breathe in this toxic smoke directly—and often. Even more troubling is that most of these workers are only teenagers. They are children who must work because their families need the money to survive. The risks to health and physical growth from the toxins released by burning plastic are frightening.

Plastic air pollution

6   When any type of plastic is burned, it releases toxic chemicals into the air. According to the US Department of Health, toxic chemicals released by burning e-waste can cause health problems such as cancer, leukemia, and asthma.

7   One of the poisons released through the burning of plastic is dioxin. It tends to stick to the waxy surface of leaves, where it can then enter the food chain. Toxins that get into the food chain will eventually be consumed by people. Residue from burning also pollutes the soil and groundwater. It can enter the food chain through crops and livestock. In addition, certain chemicals released by burning can accumulate in animal fats. When people eat meat, fish, or dairy products, they then consume the chemicals.

8   This is not just a problem for developing countries. Agricultural plastics are often burned near food sources. It is particularly important to reduce this health hazard to food production.

Watch where it goes!

9   Inspections in 2009 showed that 48 percent of waste exports from the European Union were illegal. And, in the United States, only about 10 percent of discarded computers are recycled again for use inside the United States. The United Nations estimates that 22 to 55 million tons of electronic waste are produced every year. There is clearly a need for laws to be more strongly enforced to ensure that the e-waste is disposed of responsibly. There should also be better monitoring of recycled computers, identifying where they are going and what condition they are in. Discarded computers sent overseas should actually work, to eliminate the temptation to "mine" them for metals.

Adapted from: Knight, G. (2012). *Plastic Pollution*. Chicago: Heinemann-Raintree.

English Reading for Academic Purposes 1B

Task A | Reading Comprehension Strategy: Organizing information—creating a concept map

1. Scan the passage, and with a partner discuss these questions.
   1) What is e-waste?
   2) Why do a growing number of laws prohibit the dumping of e-waste?
   3) What does the new mining industry mean?

Write your answers to the questions below

2. Read the passage again and identify the information about how discarded electronics have become a huge problem. Fill in the concept map below.

A concept map helps you organize information in a visual way. To create a concept map, write the general topic or main idea of the text in the center. Then write other key ideas around the main idea. Link the ideas with lines to show how they connect. After that, add and link additional details. Generally, ideas in the middle of a concept map are more general. Ideas further from the middle are usually smaller details.

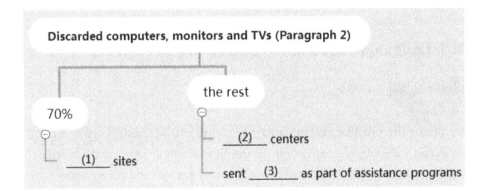

Discarded computers, monitors and TVs (Paragraph 2)

- 70%
  - ___(1)___ sites
- the rest
  - ___(2)___ centers
  - sent ___(3)___ as part of assistance programs

Unit 8　Environmental Protection | 211

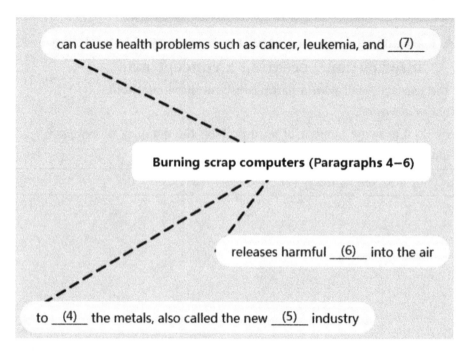

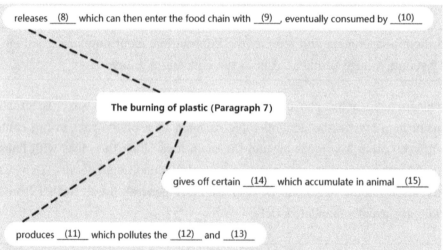

Task B | Language Spotlight: Clarifying cause and effect

Exercises

1. Some signal words can be used in a text to indicate that there is a reason and a result or cause and effect being explained. Read Paragraph 5 again and identify the cause and effect chain. Use the appropriate signals to rewrite the paragraph.

English Reading for Academic Purposes 1B

> Signals for cause and effect pattern:
>
> *to cause/to lead to/to result in/to produce/to give rise to/to bring about/ to result from/because/due to/owing to/as a consequence/as a result/ the cause of ...*

1) burning the plastic computer cases → harmful toxins into the air → workers breathing in this toxic smoke → risks to health and physical growth from the toxins being frightening
2) families needing money to survive → teenagers having to work

2. Further work on the use of signal words.
   1) Here are two possible causes for the effects listed below. Write the letters of the effects which should go with each cause. Some of the effects can be used twice. Work with a partner and use the appropriate signals to link the ideas.

Cause 1: An aging population	Effects:
Cause 2: Learning a new language	Effects:

Possible effects:

a. Travel agents offering special trips
b. Meeting interesting people
c. Feeling cut off from the world
d. Many headaches
e. Suffering from depression

f. Going to the language lab
g. New services being developed
h. Understanding others' ideas
i. More job opportunities
j. Heavy tax burden on working people

Unit 8 Environmental Protection | 213

2) Here are two effects which have multiple causes. Write the letters of the causes which you think should go with each effect. Some of the causes can be used twice. Work with a partner and use the appropriate signals to link the ideas.

Effect 1: A car is stuck in traffic.	Causes:
Effect 2: Many animals have become extinct.	Causes:

Possible causes:

    a. Smaller rain forests   e. Polluted rivers
    b. Use of chemical fertilizers   f. Wars
    c. Heavy rain   g. No petrol
    d. Broken engine   h. Too many hunters

Task C | Vocabulary Practice: Understanding words with multiple meanings

> Many words have more than one meaning. In some cases, the words may be different parts of speech; for example, a noun and a verb. In other cases, they may be different, or similar, in meaning. In each case, you may need to use a dictionary to understand a word's exact meaning.

Exercises

1. Read each of the following sentences from the passage. With a partner, decide the meaning of the underlined words according to the parts of speech or the context of the passage.

    1) However, sending electronic equipment overseas as part of assistance programs **raises** issues of its own.
        a. to lift or move sth. to a higher level
        b. to increase the amount or level of sth.
        c. to bring or collect money or people together; to manage to get or form sth.
        d. to cause or produce sth.; to make sth. appear
        e. to care for a child or young animal until it is able to take care of itself

2) When shipping containers of secondhand computers first began arriving in Ghana in the mid-2000s, the intention was to help **close** the digital **divide** with developed countries.

close:
a. to put sth. into a position so that it covers an opening; to get into this position
b. to move the parts of sth. together so that it is no longer open
c. to end or make sth. end
d. to make the work of a shop/store, etc. stop for a period of time
e. to make the distance or difference between two people or things smaller; to become smaller or narrower

divide:
f. (v.) to separate or make sth. separate into parts
g. (v.) to use different parts of your time, energy, etc. for different activities, etc.
h. (v.) to make two or more people disagree
i. (n.) a difference between two groups of people that separates them from each other
j. (n.) a line of high land that separates two systems of rivers

3) Burning the plastic computer cases **releases** harmful toxins into the air.
a. to let sb./sth. come out of a place where they have been kept or trapped
b. to stop holding sth. or stop it from being held so that it can move, fly, fall, etc. freely
c. to express feelings such as anger or worry in order to get rid of them
d. to make sth. available to the public
e. to cause gas or heat to leave its container or the substance that it was part of and enter the surrounding atmosphere or area

4) There should also be better **monitoring** of recycled computers, identifying where they are going and what condition they are in.
a. (n.) a screen that shows information from a computer
b. (n.) a piece of equipment used to check or record sth.
c. (n.) a student in a school who performs special duties, such as helping the teacher
d. (v.) to watch and check sth. over a period of time in order to see how it develops, so that you can make any necessary changes
e. (v.) to listen to telephone calls, foreign radio broadcasts, etc. in order to find out information that might be useful

5) Discarded computers sent overseas should actually work, to eliminate the temptation to "**mine**" them for metals.

a. (*pron.*) of or belonging to the person writing or speaking

b. (*n.*) a deep hole or holes under the ground where minerals such as coal, gold, etc. are dug

c. (*n.*) a type of bomb hidden under the ground or in the sea that explodes when sb./sth. touches it

d. (*v.*) to dig holes in the ground in order to find and obtain coal, diamonds, etc.

e. (*v.*) to place a bomb in an area of land or water which will explode when people or things touch it

2. With a partner, identify the words from the passage with the closest meanings below, writing them in the gaps.

1) _____ a substance or object that covers something and protects it

2) _____ helpful or kind, marked by good intentions though often producing unfortunate results

3) _____ something that is given to a person or an organization such as a charity, in order to help them; the act of giving sth. in this way

4) _____ things that are not wanted or cannot be used for their original purpose, but which have some value for the material they are made of

5) _____ material produced by or used in a reaction involving changes in atoms or molecules

6) _____ a small amount that remains after most of it has gone

7) _____ something that could be dangerous to you, your health or safety, or your plans or reputation

8) _____ a formal or official examination

9) _____ to make sure that people obey a particular law or rule

10) _____ to remove or get rid of sth./sb. completely

Task D | Critical Thinking: Further evaluating the content of the text

Discussion

Think about the following questions and discuss with your group.

1. Should developed countries ban sending computers to developing countries unless tougher rules are enforced?
2. Can anything be done to protect the children and young people forced to work as salvagers*?

3. Could anything be done to make older computers worth more than the salvageable metals inside them?

*****salvagers**: People who salvage (manage to save) computer chips for tiny amounts of gold, copper, etc.

Notes

Glossary of Unit 8

Reading 1

exceptionally

adv. used before an adjective or adverb to emphasize how strong or unusual the quality is

e. g. Exceptionally dry weather over the past year had cut agricultural production.

utensil

n. an implement, instrument, or vessel used in a household and especially a kitchen

e. g. The best carving utensil is a long, sharp and flexible knife.

durability

n. permanence by virtue of the power to resist stress or force

e. g. This factory's products are noted for their fine workmanship and durability.

adhesive

n. a substance such as glue, which is used to make things stick firmly together

e. g. Glue the mirror in with a strong adhesive.

clog

v. to block sth. or to become blocked

e. g. Within a few years the pipes began to clog up.

litter

v. to leave things in a place, making it look untidy

e. g. He had to pay a fine for littering.

flutter

v. to move lightly and quickly

e. g. The breeze made the curtains flutter.

Reading 2

prohibit

v. to stop sth. from being done or used especially by law

e. g. The prison's electric fence prohibits escape.

shipment

n. a load of goods that are sent from one place to another

e. g. This shipment is not up to your usual standards.

salvage

v. to save parts or property from a damaged ship or from a fire, etc.; to manage to rescue sth. from a difficult situation

e. g. Divers salvaged some of the sunken ship's cargo.

toxic

adj. containing poison; poisonous

e. g. Tests will be run to determine if the landfill is toxic.

temptation

n. the desire to do or have sth. that you know is bad or wrong

e. g. The dessert menu has a lot of delicious temptations.

Plastic Pollution Crisis Around the World

Much of the planet is swimming in discarded plastic, which is harming animal and possibly human health. Can it be cleaned up?

Plastic pollution has become one of the most pressing environmental issues, as rapidly increasing production of disposable plastic products overwhelms the world's ability to deal with them. Plastic pollution is most visible in developing Asian and African nations, where garbage collection systems are often inefficient or nonexistent. But the developed world, especially in countries with low recycling rates, also has trouble properly collecting discarded plastics. Plastic trash has become so ubiquitous it has prompted efforts to write a global treaty negotiated by the United Nations.

How did this happen?

Plastics made from fossil fuels are just over a century old. Production and development of thousands of new plastic products accelerated after World War II, so transforming the modern age that life without plastics would be unrecognizable today. Plastics revolutionized medicine with life-saving devices, made space travel possible, lightened cars and jets—saving fuel and pollution—and saved lives with helmets, incubators, and equipment for clean drinking water.

The conveniences plastics offer, however, led to a throw-away culture that reveals the material's dark side: today, single-use plastics account for 40 percent of the plastic produced every year. Many of these products, such as plastic bags and food wrappers, have a lifespan of mere minutes to hours, yet they may persist in the environment for hundreds of years.

Plastics by the numbers

Some key facts:
- ★ Half of all plastics ever manufactured have been made in the last 15 years.
- ★ Production increased exponentially, from 2.3 million tons in 1950 to 448 million

tons by 2015. Production is expected to double by 2050.

★ Every year, about 8 million tons of plastic waste escapes into the oceans from coastal nations. That's the equivalent of setting five garbage bags full of trash on every foot of coastline around the world.

★ Plastics often contain additives making them stronger, more flexible, and durable. But many of these additives can extend the life of products if they become litter, with some estimates ranging to at least 400 years to break down.

How plastics move around the world

Most of the plastic trash in the oceans, Earth's last sink, flows from land. Trash is also carried to sea by major rivers, which act as conveyor belts, picking up more and more trash as they move downstream. Once at sea, much of the plastic trash remains in coastal waters. But once caught up in ocean currents, it can be transported around the world.

On Henderson Island, an uninhabited atoll in the Pitcairn Group isolated halfway between Chile and New Zealand, scientists found plastic items from Russia, the United States, Europe, South America, Japan, and China. They were carried to the South Pacific by the South Pacific gyre, a circular ocean current.

Microplastics

Once at sea, sunlight, wind, and wave action break down plastic waste into small particles, often less than one-fifth of an inch across. These so-called microplastics are spread throughout the water column and have been found in every corner of the globe, from Mount Everest, the highest peak, to the Mariana Trench, the deepest trough.

Microplastics are breaking down further into smaller and smaller pieces. Plastic microfibers, meanwhile, have been found in municipal drinking water systems and drifting through the air.

Harm to wildlife

Millions of animals are killed by plastics every year, from birds to fish to other marine organisms. Nearly 700 species, including endangered ones, are known to have been affected by plastics. Nearly every species of seabird eats plastics.

Most of the deaths to animals are caused by entanglement or starvation. Seals, whales, turtles, and other animals are strangled by abandoned fishing gear or discarded six-pack rings. Microplastics have been found in more than 100 aquatic species, including fish, shrimp, and mussels destined for our dinner plates. In many cases, these tiny bits pass through the digestive system and are expelled without consequence. But plastics have also been found to have blocked digestive tracts or pierced organs, causing death. Stomachs so packed with plastics reduce the urge to eat, causing starvation.

Plastics have been consumed by land-based animals, including elephants, hyenas, zebras, tigers, camels, cattle, and other large mammals, in some cases causing death.

Tests have also confirmed liver and cell damage and disruptions to reproductive systems, prompting some species, such as oysters, to produce fewer eggs. New research shows that larval fish are eating nanofibers in the first days of life, raising new questions about the effects of plastics on fish populations.

Stemming the plastic tide

Once in the ocean, it is difficult—if not impossible—to retrieve plastic waste. Mechanical systems, such as Mr. Trash Wheel, a litter interceptor in Maryland's Baltimore Harbor, can be effective at picking up large pieces of plastic, such as foam cups and food containers, from inland waters. But once plastics break down into microplastics and drift throughout the water column in the open ocean, they are virtually impossible to recover.

The solution is to prevent plastic waste from entering rivers and seas in the first place, many scientists and conservationists—including the National Geographic Society—say. This could be accomplished with improved waste management systems and recycling, better product design that takes into account the short life of disposable packaging, and reduction in manufacturing of unnecessary single-use plastics.

Source: Parker, L. (2019, June 7). The world's plastic pollution crisis explained. *nationalgeographic.com*. Retrieved September 12, 2020, from https://www.nationalgeographic.com/environment/article/plastic-pollution.

English Reading for Academic Purposes 1B

Unit 9

Science Changes Life

Anyone who thinks science is trying to make human life easier or more pleasant is utterly mistaken. —*Albert Einstein*

What do you think about science and how does it interact with humans?

In this unit, you will have a look at issues about science and examine how it affects humans and life. You will practice reading strategies of identifying logical flowing of ideas in passage and recognizing essay structure. Also, you will learn about language and lexical features that are typically used in an academic context and will practice using them appropriately.

By the end of this unit, you will be able to:	
SKILL	TASK
identify the logical flowing of ideas	• Reading 1 • Task A
use appropriate language to refer to sources	• Reading 1 • Task B
enlarge vocabulary by synonyms	• Reading 1 • Task C
do critical thinking on relationship between AI and human life	• Reading 1 • Task D
recognize essay structure	• Reading 2 • Task A
use language for tendency	• Reading 2 • Task B
deduce the meaning of unfamiliar phrases	• Reading 2 • Task C
do critical thinking on driverless cars in real life	• Reading 2 • Task D

Reading 1

Artificial Intelligence and the Future of Humans

1   Experts say the rise of artificial intelligence will make most people better off over the next decade, but many have concerns about how advances in AI will affect what it means to be human, to be productive and to exercise free will.

2   Digital life is augmenting human capacities and disrupting eons-old human activities. Code-driven systems have spread to more than half of the world's inhabitants in ambient information and connectivity, offering previously unimagined opportunities and unprecedented threats. As emerging algorithm-driven artificial intelligence (AI) continues to spread, will people be better off than they are today?

3   Some 979 technology pioneers, innovators, developers, business and policy leaders, researchers and activists answered this question in a canvassing of experts conducted in the summer of 2018.

4   The experts predicted networked artificial intelligence will amplify human effectiveness but also threaten human autonomy, agency and capabilities.

_____ They said "smart" systems in communities, in vehicles, in buildings and utilities, on farms and in business processes will save time, money and lives, and offer opportunities for individuals to enjoy a more-customized future.

5   Many focused their optimistic remarks on health care and many possible applications of AI in diagnosing and treating patients or helping senior citizens

live fuller and healthier lives. _____
Additionally, a number of these experts predicted that AI would abet long-anticipated changes in formal and informal education systems.

⁶ Yet, most experts, regardless of whether they are optimistic or not, expressed concerns about the long-term impact of these new tools on the essential elements of being human. All respondents in this non-scientific canvassing were asked to elaborate on why they felt AI would leave people better off or not. _____
_____ The main themes they sounded about threats and remedies are outlined in the accompanying table.

AI and the future of humans: Experts express concerns and suggest solutions

CONCERNS	**Human agency:** Individuals are experiencing a loss of control over their lives	Decision-making on key aspects of digital life is automatically ceded to code-driven, "black box" tools. People lack input and do not learn the context about how the tools work. They sacrifice independence, privacy and power over choice; they have no control over these processes. This effect will deepen as automated systems become more prevalent and complex.
	Data abuse: Data use and surveillance in complex systems is designed for profit or for exercising power	Most AI tools are and will be in the hands of companies striving for profits or governments striving for power. Values and ethics are often not baked into the digital systems making people's decisions for them. These systems are globally networked and not easy to regulate or rein in.
	Job loss: The AI takeover of jobs will widen economic divides, leading to social upheaval	The efficiencies and other economic advantages of code-based machine intelligence will continue to disrupt all aspects of human work. While some expect new jobs will emerge, others worry about massive job losses, widening economic divides and social upheavals, including populist uprisings.
	Dependence lock-in: Reduction of individuals' cognitive, social and survival skills	Many see AI as augmenting human capacities but some predict the opposite—that people's deepening dependence on machine-driven networks will erode their abilities to think for themselves, take action independent of automated systems and interact effectively with others.

	Mayhem: Autonomous weapons, cybercrime and weaponized information	Some predict further erosion of traditional sociopolitical structures and the possibility of great loss of lives due to accelerated growth of autonomous military applications and the use of weaponized information, lies and propaganda to dangerously destabilize human groups. Some also fear cybercriminals' reach into economic systems.
SUGGESTED SOLUTIONS	**Global good is No.1**: Improve human collaboration across borders and stakeholder groups	Digital cooperation to serve humanity's best interests is the top priority. Ways must be found for people around the world to come to common understandings and agreements—to join forces to facilitate the innovation of widely accepted approaches aimed at tackling wicked problems and maintaining control over complex human-digital networks.
	Values-based system: Develop policies to assure AI will be directed at "humanness" and common good	Adopt a "moonshot mentality" to build inclusive, decentralized intelligent digital networks "imbued with empathy" that help humans aggressively ensure that technology meets social and ethical responsibilities. Some new level of regulatory and certification process will be necessary.
	Prioritize people: Alter economic and political systems to better help humans "race with the robots"	Reorganize economic and political systems toward the goal of expanding humans' capacities and capabilities in order to heighten human/AI collaboration and staunch trends that would compromise human relevance in the face of programmed intelligence.

7 Overall, and despite the downsides they fear, 63% of respondents in this canvassing said they are hopeful that most individuals will be mostly better off in 2030, and 37% said people will not be better off.

8 A number of the thought leaders who participated in this canvassing said humans' expanding reliance on technological systems will only go well if close attention is paid to how these tools, platforms and networks are engineered, distributed and updated. Some of the powerful, overarching answers included those from:

9 Sonia Katyal, co-director of the Berkeley Center for Law and Technology and a member of the inaugural US Commerce Department Digital Economy

Board of Advisors, predicted, "In 2030, the greatest set of questions will involve how perceptions of AI and their application will influence the trajectory of civil rights in the future. Questions about privacy, speech, the right of assembly and technological construction of personhood will all re-emerge in this new AI context, throwing into question our deepest-held beliefs about equality and opportunity for all. _____
_____ "

10   Erik Brynjolfsson, director of the MIT Initiative on the Digital Economy and author of "Machine, Platform, Crowd: Harnessing Our Digital Future", said, " AI and related technologies have already achieved superhuman performance in many areas, and there is little doubt that their capabilities will improve, probably very significantly, by 2030 … I think it is more likely than not that we will use this power to make the world a better place. For instance, we can virtually eliminate global poverty, massively reduce disease and provide better education to almost everyone on the planet. That said, AI and ML [machine learning] can also be used to increasingly concentrate wealth and power, leaving many people behind, and to create even more horrifying weapons. _____
We need to work aggressively to make sure technology matches our values. This can and must be done at all levels, from government, to business, to academia, and to individual choices."

11   Judith Donath, author of "The Social Machine, Designs for Living Online" and faculty fellow at Harvard University's Berkman Klein Center for Internet & Society, commented, " _____ "
At home, parents will engage skilled bots to help kids with homework and catalyze dinner conversations. At work, bots will run meetings. A bot confidant will be considered essential for psychological well-being, and we'll increasingly turn to such companions for advice ranging from what to wear to whom to marry.

Source: Anderson, J. & Lee, R. (2018, December 10). Artificial intelligence and the future of humans. *Pew Research Center*. Retrieved May 10, 2020, from https://www.pewresearch.org/internet/2018/12/10/artificial-intelligence-and-the-future-of-humans/.

Task A | Reading Comprehension Strategy: Identifying logical flowing of ideas

> **How to identify the logical relationship of ideas**
>
> Ideas usually flow in some kind of logical way in a text. The logical flowing of ideas can be achieved by certain lexical, grammatical devices or context.

Exercise

Read through the passage and identify to which part of the passage each of the following sentences missing from the passage belongs. Write the number of the paragraph in brackets before the sentence.

(   ) a. Many shared deep worries, and many also suggested pathways toward solutions.

(   ) b. Neither outcome is inevitable, so the right question is not "What will happen?" but "What will we choose to do?"

(   ) c. They spoke of the wide-ranging possibilities; that computers might match or even exceed human intelligence and capabilities on tasks such as complex decision-making, reasoning and learning, sophisticated analytics and pattern recognition, visual acuity, speech recognition and language translation.

(   ) d. By 2030, most social situations will be facilitated by bots—intelligent-seeming programs that interact with us in human-like ways.

(   ) e. Who will benefit and who will be disadvantaged in this new world depends on how broadly we analyze these questions today, for the future.

(   ) f. They were also enthusiastic about AI's role in contributing to broad public-health programs built around massive amounts of data that may be captured in the coming years about everything from personal genomes to nutrition.

Task B | Language Spotlight: Present participle as adverbial of result

1. Read the following sentence taken from the passage and try to rewrite the sentence by filling in the blanks.

   "*Code-driven systems have spread to more than half of the world's inhabitants in ambient information and connectivity, offering previously unimagined opportunities and unprecedented threats.*"

The sentence can be rewritten like this:

"Code-driven systems have spread to more than half of the world's inhabitants in ambient information and connectivity, _____ _____ previously unimagined opportunities and unprecedented threats."

> In original sentence, the part "*offering previously unimagined opportunities and unprecedented threats*" is a present participle used as an adverbial of result. We may rewrite the sentence by replacing this part with a nonrestrictive attributive clause.

2. Identify another example of present participle used as an adverbial of result in the passage and rewrite it.

_____

3. Rewrite the following sentences with present participles used as adverbials.

   1) AI and ML (machine learning) can also be used to increasingly concentrate wealth and power, leaving many people behind.

   _____

   2) AI will help mankind to manage resources like energy, transport, more efficiently, making people live safer and healthier.

   _____

   3) AI machines should remain at the level of tools or, at most, assistants, always keeping the human in the loop.

   _____

Task C | Vocabulary Practice: Enlarging vocabulary by synonyms

> A **synonym** is a word or expression that has the same or almost the same meaning as another word or expression. In English, a language known for its enormous vocabulary, most words have synonyms. For example, the word "enormous" has many synonyms: huge, massive, giant, immense, and the list goes on. It's a great way to build vocabulary by synonyms.

1. Replace the underlined words in the sentences which are taken from the passage with words given in the box. Change the word form where necessary.

explain	user-defined	solution	increase	extend

Unit 9 Science Changes Life | 229

1) Digital life is <u>augmenting</u> human capacities and disrupting eons-old human activities.

2) The experts predicted networked artificial intelligence will <u>amplify</u> human effectiveness but also threaten human autonomy, agency and capabilities.

3) They said "smart" systems in communities, in vehicles, in buildings and utilities, on farms and in business processes will save time, money and lives and offer opportunities for individuals to enjoy a more-<u>customized</u> future.

4) All respondents in this non-scientific canvassing were asked to <u>elaborate</u> on why they felt AI would leave people better off or not.

5) The main themes they sounded about threats and <u>remedies</u> are outlined in the accompanying table.

2. Complete the following sentences using the words in the box from the above activity.

1) Based on the individual requirement, even this service can be _____.

2) She went on to _____ her argument.

3) The recent speech of the president _____ tensions in the Near East.

4) Holding copyright provides the only legal _____ against unauthorized copying.

5) This will _____ the impact of our activities and our resources.

Task D | Critical Thinking: Relationship between AI and human life

1. Work in groups, and have a further discussion on the following questions:

1) AI is made up of a complex set of different technologies. This means that as the field grows and evolves, we'll begin to see more terms being used to describe what the technology does, such as "Artificial Neural Networks". What other common AI terms do you know?

2) Artificial intelligence is a tool, and like many tools, its power can be for good or evil. Think about a hammer. It can be used for wonderful things, like building a home, but it can also be used to hurt someone else. In what way can AI be beneficial or dangerous for humans?

3) Because of AI, computers can now learn to do huge amounts of tasks and activities that used to require human intelligence. The more data the AI has, the better results it can produce.

4) One positive result of this is that AI will make our lives easier in certain areas in which we need to analyze data. Try to give an example in such areas of life as health care, agriculture, business and industry.

5) How would you apply AI in your area of interest?
6) AI has made many traditional jobs disappear, what are they? AI has also created many new jobs. What are they? What job created by AI would you like to take in the future?
2. Take notes in the following box and make a written report on the results of the above discussion.

Notes

Reading 2

Surprising Ways How Driverless Cars Will Change Our Future

¹ Most people would agree that driverless cars are the future. With the recent leaps and bounds made in the self-driving car industry, very few people would be bold enough to dispute the fact that these cars will reduce the number of road accident fatalities. Research has shown that the number of US deaths resulting from road accidents could be reduced by more than 90% by the year 2050 because of self-driving cars.

² However, this is not the only effect driverless cars will have on our future. Cars and automobiles, in general, are a huge part of our daily lives and society in general. Surprisingly, as humans we are prone to getting angry as soon as we are behind the wheel. So now the question becomes "Will driverless cars make us nicer people?"

³ Such a radical change in the automobile industry will have far-reaching effects on every other aspect of our lives. If we fully adopt driverless cars, here is how things will change.

⁴ It is expensive to own and maintain a personal vehicle. Driverless cars come with the possibility of cheap and convenient transport. Ride services like Uber will probably own fleets of driverless cars, and without the option of human drivers to pay, the running costs of such a fleet would be ridiculously low. Self-driving electric cars running on renewable energy will cost almost nothing to operate. If you can summon them and get to your destination in just a few minutes, what would you need your own car for?

☐

⁵ Driverless cars can reduce harmful emissions by up to 60%. Furthermore, these cars can be programmed to maximize the potential reductions, which is amazing news for the environmentally conscious and anyone who wants to leave a minimum impact on Mother Earth.

☐

⁶ Today, cities are designed for cars. Roads and highways have taken over, and cities have become less and less pedestrian-friendly. The advent of driverless cars could bring a shift to this phenomenon, reverting city design back to being of and for the people. More precise driverless cars mean narrower streets, with larger spaces for pedestrians. Fewer cars mean fewer traffic jams.

⁷ Crossing roads will also be easier because driverless cars are more considerate and reasonable than angry human drivers. Amenities such as traffic lights and parking garages would also go the way of the dodo. Wouldn't it be nice to have parks instead of those ugly parking lots?

☐

⁸ Today's cars are not user-friendly for the elderly or disabled, or anyone else who may have difficulty getting around. Paratransit services with wheelchair accommodation—or even hospital bed accommodation—and cars with Braille buttons will be normal. And the smart driverless car will know how to find the easiest place for its passengers to board or alight from, making their lives easier.

☐

⁹ Not having to drive means you can sit in your car and work on your way to the office. You can also choose to make the driverless car your office, driving around to clients and having meetings on the go. The fact that we have driverless cars means that vans, trucks, and buses can also be driverless. These can be converted into actual offices or stores. You can have a business model where clients order up a service and it drives to them.

¹⁰ This model is perfect for the majority of businesses, including gyms,

restaurants, clothing stores, and even translation companies. The driverless vehicle would park in front of the customer's house for an hour or so, then move on to the next customer. This would totally revolutionize how business is conducted.

☐

¹¹ The need for a short commute to work is one of the main reasons why people live close to towns. If people do not need to drive to work, they would be more inclined to live further away and just relax on the commute to and from work, without the craziness of traffic jams.

Source: Elezaj, R. (2018, October). Surprising ways how driverless cars will change our future. *Machine Design*. Retrieved Oct 20, 2020, from https://www.meachinedesign.com/mechanical-motion-systems/article/21837191/surprising-ways-how-driverless-cars-will-change-our-future.

Task A | Reading Comprehension Strategy: Recognizing essay structure

An essay is generally organized in a logical way. You can comprehend an essay better and faster if you can recognize the essay structure by noticing some structure features like headings or sub-headings.

Exercises

1. Read through the passage and fill the following headings missing from the passage in the correct boxes.
   1) The Evolution of Urban Centers
   2) Living Arrangements
   3) Fewer People Will Own Cars
   4) More Independence for the Physically Challenged
   5) Mobile Businesses
   6) Reduced Emissions
   7) Lower Deaths Rate of Road Accidents
2. Answer the following questions by identifying specific information from the passage,

using the answers in the above activity about headings to help you locate the right part quickly.

1) What will deaths rate caused by road accidents be like in 2050?
2) What are the two factors related to driverless cars that make fewer people own cars?
3) To what extent can driverless cars reduce harmful emissions?
4) With driverless cars, whom will city be friendly for?
5) In what way will the driverless cars make the life of the disabled or old easier?
6) How will the driverless cars make the model of mobile business possible?
7) What changes of life arrangements will be caused by driverless cars?

Task B | Language Spotlight: Differences between expressions of tendency

1. Look at the following two sentences taken from the passage and pay attention to the underlined expressions.
   1) Surprisingly, as humans we <u>are prone to</u> getting angry as soon as we are behind the wheel.
   2) If people do not need to drive to work, they would be more <u>inclined to</u> live further away …

> Both "prone to" and "inclined to" have pretty much the same meaning. "Prone to" is used to indicate that someone is likely to do something, apt to have something. "inclined to" means "tending or disposed toward something".
>
> Slight though it may be, the difference still exists. "prone to" is more incidental and possibly more negative. Someone prone to doing something might not be aware they do it often ("He is prone to running late.") or it might be something they don't have control over it. And that "inclined to" is more intentional and conveys the idea of an action or decision made by the person, for example, "I'm inclined to accept the truth." or "She is inclined to go home."
>
> As for the usage, "prone to" is usually followed by noun or gerund of verb, while "inclined to" is often followed by base form of verb.

2. Complete the following sentences by filling in the blanks with proper words about tendency.

1) For all her experience, she was still _____ to nerves.
2) They'll be more _____ to listen if you don't shout.
3) Working without a break makes you more _____ to error.
4) Toad was not _____ to give in all at once.
5) Tired drivers were found to be particularly _____ to ignoring warning signs.
6) Nobody felt _____ to argue with Smith.

Task C | Vocabulary Practice: Deducing the meaning of unfamiliar phrases

1. Try to deduce the meaning of the following phrases 1) –5) by looking at the context from the passage and match them with the given meanings a) –e).
   1) leaps and bounds   a) take control
   2) behind the wheel   b) go from one place to another
   3) take over   c) great improvement or rapid progress
   4) go the way of the dodo   d) fall out of common practice or use
   5) get around   e) driving or in control of vehicle

2. Try to complete the following sentences by filling in the blanks with phrases from the above activity.
   1) The army is threatening to _____ if civil unrest continues.
   2) It is difficult for Gail to _____ since she broke her leg.
   3) Crash rates are the highest during a teen's first few months _____.
   4) Wireless banking and trading is growing in _____.
   5) If you can't offer speed and quality, your company is destined to _____.

Task D | Critical Thinking: Driverless cars in real life

Discussion

1. Work in groups, and have a further discussion on the following questions:
   1) Are governments and law enforcement ready for self-driving cars?
   2) What changes do cities need to make to integrate self-driving car technology into their transportation network?
   3) How does the technology deal with situations that would currently involve decisions based on individual politeness, for example, stopping to allow pedestrians to cross a road or allowing other drivers out of a junction?
   4) Collection of data—including personal information about the trips its owner

makes is greatly needed for the technology of driverless cars. To whom will all this data belong? The owner of the car? The manufacturer? Should the police be able to demand this data in the event of an accident? What about insurers?

2. Take notes in the following box and make a written report on the results of the above discussion.

Notes

Glossary of Unit 9

Reading 1

augment
v. to enlarge or increase
e. g. In other words, we need to look at the ways in which machines can augment human labor rather than replace it.

ambient
adj. relating to the immediate surroundings of something
e. g. Ambient radiation is much weaker.

innovator
n. someone who helps to open up a new line of research or technology or art
e. g. America has huge advantages as an innovator.

agency
n. the state of being in action or exerting power
e. g. The movies could be an agency moulding the values of the public.

remark
n. a statement that expresses a personal opinion or belief
e. g. I decided to treat his remark as a joke.

abet
v. to assist or encourage, usually in some wrongdoing
e. g. He wouldn't throw the stone if those boys did not abet him.

elaborate
v. to add details, as to an account or idea; to clarify the meaning of discourse in a learned way, usually in writing
e. g. She elaborated on the main ideas in her paper.

cede
v. to give over; to surrender or relinquish to the physical control of another
e. g. The debater refused to cede the point to her opponent.

strive
v. to exert much effort or energy
e. g. Don't strive merely for the quantity of production.

erode
v. to become ground down or worse
e. g. Her confidence eroded.

collaboration
n. act of working jointly
e. g. It was a collaboration that produced extremely useful results.

overarching
adj. being central or dominant
e. g. The report's overarching message is optimistic and encouraging.

Reading 2

bold
adj. fearless and daring

e. g. Big successful moves need <u>bold</u>, masterful managers.

dispute

v. to have a disagreement over something

e. g. The two sides are locked into a bitter <u>dispute</u>.

radical

adj. important and great in degree

e. g. The country needs a calm period without <u>radical</u> change.

far-reaching

adj. having a great influence on a great number of things

e. g. The economy is in danger of collapse unless <u>far-reaching</u> reforms are implemented.

pedestrian

n. a person who is walking, especially in a town or city, rather than travelling in a vehicle

e. g. Whether a driver or a <u>pedestrian</u>, always check on local traffic regulations.

considerate

adj. showing concern for the rights and feelings of others

e. g. It was very <u>considerate</u> of him to wait.

alight

v. to get out of vehicle after a trip

e. g. Passengers for Lanzhou <u>alight</u> at Nanjing.

convert

v. to change into a different form

e. g. It takes 15 minutes to <u>convert</u> the plane into a car by removing the wings and the tail.

commute

v. to travel back and forth regularly, as between one's place of work and home

e. g. People are prepared to <u>commute</u> long distances if they are desperate for work.

What Is AI Technology and How Is It Used?

Artificial intelligence or AI is a popular buzzword you've probably heard or read about. Articles about robots, technology, and the digital age may fill your head when you think about the term AI. But what is it really, and how is it used?

Artificial intelligence is a technological advancement that involves programming technology to problem solve. Artificial intelligence is often talked about in conjunction with machine learning or deep learning and big data. This guide will dive deeper into what artificial intelligence is, how it's used, and what we can expect from it in the future.

What is AI?

The definition of artificial intelligence is the theory and development of computer programs that are able to do tasks and solve problems that usually require human intelligence. Things like visual perception, speech recognition, decision-making, and word translation are all things that would normally need human intelligence, but now computer programs are able to use their intelligence and capability to solve these tasks.

This type of intelligence was born in June of 1965 where a group of scientists and mathematicians met at Dartmouth to discuss the idea of a computer that could actually think. They didn't know what to call it or how it would work, but their conversations there created the spark that ignited artificial intelligence. Since the " Dartmouth workshop", as it is called, there have been highs and lows for the development of this intelligence. Some years went by where the idea of developing an intelligent computer was abandoned, and little to no work was done on this kind of intelligence at all. And in recent years, a flurry of work has been done developing and integrating this exciting intelligent technology into daily lives.

How does artificial intelligence differ from human intelligence?

So how is AI different from human intelligence? Artificial intelligence and the algorithms that make this intelligence run are designed by humans, and while the computer can learn and adapt or grow from its surroundings, at the end of the day it was created by humans. Human intelligence has a far greater capacity for multitasking, memories, social interactions, and self-awareness. Intelligence that is artificial doesn't have an IQ making it very different from humans and human intelligence. There are so many facets of thought and decision making that artificial intelligence simply can't master—computing feelings just isn't anything that we can train a machine to do, no matter how smart it is. You can't automate multitasking or create autonomous relationships. Cognitive learning and machine learning will always be unique and separate from each other. While AI applications can run quickly, and be more objective and accurate, its capability stops at being able to replicate human intelligence. Human thought encompasses so much more that a machine simply can't be taught, no matter how intelligent it is or what formulas you use.

How does AI work?

While it's one thing to know what AI is, it's another to understand the underlying functions. Artificial intelligence operates by processing data through advanced algorithms. It combs large data sets with its algorithms, learning from the patterns or features in the data. There are many theories and subfields in AI systems including:

Machine learning. Machine learning uses neural networks to find hidden insights from data, without being programmed for what to look for or what to conclude. Machine learning is a common way for programs to find patterns and increase their intelligence over time.

Deep learning. Deep learning utilizes huge neural networks with many layers, taking advantage of its size to process huge amounts of data with complex patterns. Deep learning is an element of machine learning, just with larger data sets and more layers.

Cognitive computing. Cognitive computing has a goal for a human-like interaction with machines. Think robots that can see and hear, and then respond as a human would.

Computer vision. In AI, computer vision utilizes pattern recognition and deep learning to understand a picture or video. This means the machine can look around and take pictures or videos in real time, and interpret the surroundings.

The overall goal of AI is to make software that can learn about an input, and explain a result with its output. Artificial intelligence gives human-like interactions, but won't be replacing humans anytime soon.

How is AI used?

Artificial intelligence is being used in hundreds of ways all around us. It has changed our world and made our lives more convenient and interesting. Some of the uses of AI you may know include:

Voice recognition. Most people know to call out for Siri when they need directions, or to ask their smart home Alexa to set a timer. This technology is a form of artificial intelligence. Machine learning helps Siri, Alexa, and other voice recognition devices learn about you and your preferences, helping it know how to help you. These tools also utilize artificial intelligence to pull in answers to your questions or perform the tasks you ask.

Self-driving cars. Machine learning and visual recognition are used in autonomous vehicles to help the car understand its surroundings and be able to react accordingly. Facial recognition and biometric systems help self-driving cars recognize people and keep them safe. These cars can learn and adapt to traffic patterns, signs, and more.

Chatbots. Many companies are utilizing artificial intelligence to strengthen their customer service teams. Chatbots can interact with customers and answer generic questions without needing to use a real human's time. They can learn and adapt to certain responses, get more information to help them produce a different output, and more. A certain word can trigger them to put out a certain definition as a response. This expert system can give a human-level of interaction to customers.

Online shopping. Online shopping systems utilize algorithms to learn more about your preferences and predict what you'll want to shop for. They can then put those items right in front of you, helping them grab your attention quickly. Amazon and other retailers are constantly working their algorithms to learn more about you and what you might buy.

Streaming services. When you sit down to watch your favorite TV show or listen to your favorite music, you may get other suggestions that seem interesting to you. That's artificial intelligence at work! It learns about your preferences and uses algorithms to process all the TV shows, movies, or music it has and finds patterns to give you suggestions.

Healthcare technology. AI is playing a huge role in healthcare technology as new tools to diagnose, develop medicine, monitor patients, and more are all being utilized. The technology can learn and develop as it is used, learning more about the patient or the medicine, and adapt to get better and improve as time goes on.

Factory and warehouse systems. Shipping and retail industries will never be the same thanks to AI-related software. Systems that automate the entire shipping process and learn as they go are making things work more quickly and more efficiently. These entire systems are transforming how warehouses and factories run, making them more safe and productive.

Educational tools. Things like plagiarism checkers and citation finders can help educators and students utilize artificial intelligence to enhance papers and research. The artificial intelligence systems can read the words used, and use their databases to research everything they know in the blink of an eye. It allows them to check spelling, grammar, for plagiarized content, and more.

There are many other uses of AI all around us every day, technology is advancing at a rapid pace and is continually changing how we live.

Source: What is AI technology and how is it used? (2020, March 31). *Western Governors University.* Retrieved May 11, 2020, fromhttps://www.wgu.edu/blog/what-ai-technology-how-used2003.html.

Unit 10

Illness and Disease

Illness and disease have always been a controversial issue in the society. As a college student, it is advisable to understand the current medical affairs. In this unit, students will discuss two different essays on antibiotics resistance, which is a hot topic in medical industry. Through reading these two texts, students will practice two different prediction skills, two different reading skills and two different critical thinking skills. Vocabulary related to antibiotics resistance will also be acquired.

By the end of this unit, you will be able to:	
SKILL	TASK
do speed reading by chunk reading	• Reading 1 • Task A
use causal collocations	• Reading 1 • Task B
learn medical words by word splash	• Reading 1 • Task C
distinguish facts from opinions	• Reading 1 • Task D
do speed reading by skipping unknown words	• Reading 2 • Task A
choose the right level of formality	• Reading 2 • Task B
learn words used to describe negative effects	• Reading 2 • Task C
understand inferences and evidence	• Reading 2 • Task D

READING & CRITICAL THINKING

Reading 1

Pre-reading activity

Prediction Strategies: Noticing the Text

Readers start to predict by noticing the title, author and illustrations, photos or artwork. For example, if you see that the title of a story is "The Black Cat", you might predict that the story is about a bad luck cat. When you see that the story is by Edgar Allan Poe, you can clarify that prediction because now you know the story is likely in the horror or suspense genre. Then you notice that a picture of the cat includes a man with an ax, and you make an even more specific prediction: The story will feature a man who tries to kill an unlucky black cat.

Read the title and predict the content of the essay.

Notes

Cold Comfort

¹ Not so long ago, many of us resisted separating the glass, cans, and paper out of our garbage. What a hassle. Today, of course, every second-grader knows that the world's resources are limited and that recycling helps preserve them. We act locally, while thinking globally. It's time to bring the same consciousness to health care as we face a growing medical crisis: the loss of antibiotic effectiveness against common bacterial illnesses. By personally refusing—or not demanding—antibiotics for viral illnesses they won't cure, we can each take a step toward prolonging overall antibiotic effectiveness.

² Media reports have likely made you aware of this problem, but they have neglected the implications. Your brother catches a cold that turns into a sinus infection. His doctor treats him with antibiotics, but the bacteria are resistant to all of them. The infection enters his bloodstream—a condition known as septicemia—and a few days later, your brother dies. (Septicemia is what killed Muppets creator Jim Henson a few years ago.) Or instead of a cold, he has an infected cut that won't heal, or any other common bacterial disease, such as an ear or prostate infection.

³ Far-fetched? It's not. The antibiotics crisis is real. Consider Streptococcus pneumoniae: This common bacterium often causes post-flu pneumonia. (Pneumonia and influenza combined are the country's sixth leading cause of death, killing 82,500 Americans in 1996.) Before 1980, less than 1 percent of S. pneumoniae samples showed any resistance to penicillin. As of last May, researchers at the Naval Medical Center in San Diego discovered that 22 percent of S. pneumoniae samples were highly resistant to it, with another 15 percent moderately so. And the most recent statistics from the Sentry Antimicrobial Surveillance Program, which monitors bacterial resistance at 70 medical centers in the US, Canada, Europe, and South America, show that 44 percent of S. pneumoniae samples in the US are highly resistant, and worldwide, resistance is at an all-time high (55 percent).

4   Strains of S. pneumoniae are also now resistant to tetracycline, erythromycin, clindamycin, chloramphenicol, and several other antibiotics. And there's a "plausible risk" that we'll run out of options for treating other types of pneumonia as well, according to infectious disease expert Joshua Lederberg of Rockefeller University in New York. The not-too-distant future promises the potential failure of medicine's ability to treat a broad range of bacterial infections—from urinary tract infections to meningitis to tuberculosis.

5   Bacterial resistance to antibiotics is a direct outgrowth of the overuse of these drugs. In classic Darwinian fashion, the more doctors prescribe antibiotics, the more likely it is for some lucky bacterium blessed with a minor genetic variation to survive antibiotic assault—and pass its resistance along to its offspring. The solution is obvious: Doctors should prescribe antibiotics only as a last resort.

6   This strategy works. In the early 1990s, Finnish public health authorities responded to rising bacterial resistance to erythromycin by discouraging its use as a first-line treatment for certain infections. From 1991 to 1992, erythromycin consumption per capita dropped 43 percent. By 1996, bacterial resistance to the antibiotic had been cut almost in half. But American doctors are doing a spectacularly lousy job of keeping their pens off their prescription pads, most notably by prescribing antibiotics for the common cold and other upper respiratory tract infections (URIs). Data from the National Ambulatory Medical Care Survey show that bronchitis and URIs account for a third of the nation's antibiotic prescriptions. Antibiotics treat only bacterial infections and are completely powerless against viral illnesses. Every doctor knows this. Yet, according to a recent study by Dr. Ralph Gonzalez, an assistant professor of medicine at the University of Colorado Health Sciences Center in Denver, when adults consult physicians for URIs and the bronchitis that often follows them, more than half walk out with a prescription for an antibiotic. If doctors simply stopped prescribing antibiotics for conditions they know don't respond to them, we'd instantly be well on our way to minimizing antibiotic resistance.

7   Why are doctors so ready to prescribe antibiotics? Physicians are quick to

blame the public. Patients, they say, demand antibiotics, and doctors are so terrified of malpractice suits they prescribe them to keep their customers happy and their lawyers at bay.

8   There's another side to the story: Doctors are trained that there's a pill for every ill (or there should be). All of their medical education conspires to make an antibiotic prescription their knee-jerk reaction to any infection, which may or may not have a bacterial cause.

9   In addition, prescribing antibiotics is the doctors' path of least resistance. It's easier than taking the time to explain that antibiotics are worthless against viral infections, and to recommend rest, fluids, and Vitamin C—or, God forbid, an herbal, homeopathic, Chinese, or other complementary treatment. Most medical practices schedule patients at 15-minute intervals. Rather than doing what they know is right for public health, it's much quicker for doctors to whip out the prescription pad and send people on their merry, albeit misinformed way.

10   In a better world, medical education would be less drug-oriented and the health care system would encourage doctors to take the time to be effective health educators. But even in our imperfect world, some basic health education can help prevent frivolous antibiotic use from boomeranging.

11   Like our doctors, we Americans have been socialized into believing that antibiotics are miracle drugs that can cure just about everything. They aren't, and they don't. We've also been trained to think that colds and their lingering coughs should clear up in a few days. They usually don't—even if you load up on cold formulas that promise to make all symptoms magically vanish. A study by University of Virginia professor of medicine Jack Gwaltney, one of the nation's top cold researchers, shows that nearly one-third of adults with colds are still coughing after 10 days. Meanwhile, according to a recent survey by researchers at Louisiana State University Medical Center in New Orleans, after just five days of cold symptoms, 61 percent of adults are ready to head for their doctors—and ask for unnecessary antibiotic prescriptions.

¹² My fellow Americans, the next time you feel a cold coming on, mark your calendar. Unless you start coughing up lots of green sputum or develop unusual symptoms—for example, a fever that does not respond to aspirin, acetaminophen (Tylenol), or ibuprofen (Advil, Motrin)—think twice about calling your doctor before two weeks have passed.

¹³ What I do instead is, from the moment I feel the infection coming on, I drink lots of hot fluids, take 500 to 1,000 milligrams of Vitamin C four times a day, suck on a zinc lozenge every two waking hours, and mix half a teaspoon of tincture of echinacea, an immune-boosting herb, into juice or tea three times a day. Reliable studies show that these approaches reduce the severity and duration of colds. If you develop a persistent cough at the tail end of your cold, keep taking Vitamin C and try an over-the-counter cough suppressant containing dextromethorphan.

¹⁴ If we hope to preserve antibiotic effectiveness, it's up to us, the public, to convince doctors to prescribe these drugs only when they're necessary. This from-the-bottom-up approach is nothing new. Health consumers have taken the lead in showing doctors the value of fitness, nutrition, and alternative therapies. It's time we get serious about antibiotics.

Source: Sloane, Stephen E. (2020, September). Cold comfort. *Health and Food*, pp 38–40.

Post-reading activity

Task A | Reading Comprehension Strategy: Chunk reading

Chunk reading is considered as an effective reading skill. Good readers always "chunk" when they read. They usually read a group of meaningful words rather than a lot of separate words. Then what is a meaningful phrase, or chunk? Please compare the following two examples:

A. *Effective reader in Chinese*

B. *Reader chunk as*

Example A is a meaningful phrase because it makes sense alone.

Example B is not a meaningful phrase because it does not make sense alone.

Chunk reading will not only help readers have a better understanding of a passage, but also make them take in more information at a time. Please compare the following two examples:

A. Each chunk/should be a phrase/that makes sense/by itself.

(slower readers)

B. Each chunk should be a phrase/that makes sense by itself.

(faster readers)

As we can see, faster readers tend to acquire more information when they do chunk reading

Exercises

1. Read the first paragraph.

Not so long ago, many of us resisted separating the glass, cans, and paper out of our garbage. What a hassle. Today, of course, every second-grader knows that the world's resources are limited and that recycling helps preserve them. We act locally, while thinking globally. It's time to bring the same consciousness to health care as we face a growing medical crisis: the loss of antibiotic effectiveness against common bacterial illnesses. By personally refusing—or not demanding—antibiotics for viral illnesses they won't cure, we can each take a step toward prolonging overall antibiotic effectiveness.

2. Now read the paragraph aloud to another student and then let him or her read it to you.
3. Read the same paragraph divided into meaningful phrases.

Not so long ago	many of us
resisted separating the glass	cans and paper
out of our garbage	What a hassle
Today	of course
every second-grader	knows that
the world's resources	are limited
and that	recycling helps preserve them
We act locally	while thinking globally
It's time to	bring the same consciousness
to health care	as we face
a growing medical crisis the loss of	antibiotic effectiveness
against common bacterial illnesses	By personally refusing
or not demanding	antibiotics
for viral illnesses	they won't cure
we can each	take a step toward
prolonging overall antibiotic effectiveness	

4. Now read the paragraph aloud to another student, pausing very briefly after each phrase. It it easier to understand the paragraph with or without the division into phrases?

Task B | Language Spotlight: Identifying cause and effect expressions

Work with a partner. Underline the cause and effect expressions in the following sentences chosen from *Longman Dictionary of Contemporary English*.

1) Breast cancer is a leading cause of death for American women in their 40s.
2) Heavy traffic is causing delays on the freeway.
3) What caused you to change your mind?
4) The excessive heat was responsible for their deaths.
5) The Internet has brought about enormous changes in society.
6) The decision is likely to result in a large number of job losses.
7) We are still dealing with problems resulting from errors made in the past.
8) A poor diet in childhood can lead to health problems later in life.

9) His actions could lead to him losing his job.
10) Alcohol contributes to 100,000 deaths a year in the US.

Task C | Vocabulary Practice: Learning medical words by a word splash

What is a *word splash*? A word splash is created by a group of words related to a topic. Work with a partner, and write or type a paragraph that connects those 4 – 8 words in the following picture related to the offered topic.

Notes

Task D | Critical Thinking: Distinguishing facts from opinions

When you read about events, you must distinguish the facts that have already occurred from an individual's opinion or judgment about those events.

A fact is something that can be proven true by reliable evidence. An opinion, in contrast, is defined as evaluation, impression or estimation of the value or worth of a person or thing. Opinions normally can not be proven.

Follow these guidelines to help you distinguish facts from opinions:
- Evaluate the sources for all information.
- Read carefully for word clues. Does the writer use positive or negative descriptions of people or events? Some words indicating opinions are *I believe*, *I think*, *should*, *best*, *worst*, *all*, *everyone*, and *hardest*.
- Whether the event is described could be observed or must be implied. For example, is the description a statement or a thought?
- Compare multiple sources about the same event, and note how they are the same and how they are different. These differences may indicate opinions.

Exercise

Read the following statements. Fill in the blank with an "O" or an "F" to indicate whether the statement is an opinion or a fact.

1) _____ Antibiotics have saved the lives of millions of people by eliminating the pathogenic bacteria that are the cause of vast majority of infectious diseases.
2) _____ We should remember that human intestines naturally contain around 100 trillion bacteria that are not only useful but essential for our well-being.
3) _____ Using and especially overusing antibiotics may throw the delicate balance out of whack, causing a wide range of syndromes ranging from annoying to fatal.
4) _____ To put it simply, the more we use antibiotics, the more resistant bacteria grow.
5) _____ As a result, physicians are forced to prescribe either more potent and therefore toxic antibiotics, or larger doses of them.
6) _____ This poisons the patient and makes the bacteria even more resistant to treatment.
7) _____ Today the world healthcare industry is growing more and more alarmed by

the perspective of post-antibiotic world terrorized by "superbugs"—pathogens that are no longer treatable by antibiotics.

8) _____ A study by University of Virginia professor of medicine Jack Gwaltney, one of the nation's top cold researchers, shows that nearly one-third of adults with colds are still coughing after 10 days.

Notes

READING & CRITICAL THINKING

Reading 2

Pre-reading activity

Prediction Skills: Prediction Chart

To stay focused, it may help to write down your initial predictions before you start reading. As you get involved with the text, you can start clarifying those predictions using evidence in the story. As a helpful strategy, you may want to make a chart with three columns:
- ➢ one for your original prediction;
- ➢ one for evidence you found that helps you revise or clarify the prediction;
- ➢ one for the new prediction based on the clues you have found.

The chart will give you a permanent record of what was your thinking that led to understanding the text. Work with partners and fill in the prediction charts.

Prediction Charts

What I predict the text will be about	The clues that are used to predict	What the text really talks about

The Growing Global Threat of Antibiotics Resistance

¹ Antibiotics have been one of humanity's success stories for hundreds of years, being responsible both for saving the lives of millions of patients and for helping scientists to take enormous steps in the fields of medical and surgical treatment. But this success has come at a price. The growing resistance of many bacterial strains to the curative effects of antibiotics is such a concern that it has been referred to, in some quarters, as the greatest threat to our continued existence on earth. We have become careless, it is argued, not only in our reliance on the quick fix of medicine if we feel even slightly under the weather, but also in taking the availability of antibiotics for granted, using them incorrectly, not following the prescribed dosage. This has given rise to a new form of super bacteria, a type which is able to fight off antibiotic treatment with ease.

² Although their resistance to antibiotics has been built up over a long period of time, bacteria actually replicate extraordinarily quickly, and any resistance developed is also duplicated as they divide. In addition, those bacteria carrying resistance genes happen to spread those genes further via "horizontal gene transfer", a process whereby one bacterium passes on the resistance gene from another without even needing to be its parent. What makes the spread of these strains more difficult to control is that it occurs in a cyclical process. In the case of humans, when a person becomes infected and the resistant bacteria set up home in the gut, the sufferer has two choices: look for help or stay at home. In seeking medical assistance, whether through an appointment to visit their local doctor, or taking themselves to hospital, they contaminate other patients, later to be discharged and sent home. The resistant bacteria then spread out into the local community. This is also the end result if the infected person decides not to seek any medical assistance at all: they keep the bacteria at home and allow them to breed without treatment.

³ Livestock also play their part in dispersing these newly evolved, bullet-proof microorganisms into the food chain. These resilient bacteria do not discriminate between man and beast, and so animals play host to the very

same bacteria as are found in humans, with the end result that our farms and abattoirs have become breeding grounds for inter-species infection. In fact, even after slaughter, these bacteria can easily survive on animal carcasses, remaining alive and reproducing until the point of purchase and beyond, eventually invading our systems when we ingest the flesh as infected meat. So is the answer simply to become a vegetarian? Sadly not. The very same resistant bacteria will leave a host animal's gut in the form of faces, which are employed in agriculture as manure to support food crops. From there, the wheat, maize and corn that are grown for human consumption transport the bacteria into our bodies. There really is no escape.

4   That said, there is always something that can be done to try and minimize any risk, however much of a lost cause it might seem. In 2014, after accumulating data from 114 countries, the World Health Organization (WHO) issued a set of guidelines intended to tackle the increasing problem of resistance. Doctors and pharmacists were advised to avoid prescribing and dispensing antibiotics as much and as often as possible. Only when treatment is utterly necessary should they resort to doing so, while the greatest of care should be taken to ensure that the antibiotics they provide are the correct ones to treat the illness. In turn, the general public must play their part by only taking antibiotics as prescribed by a doctor, as well as making sure they see out the full course, even if they feel better before the antibiotics are finished. Additionally, they should never share their medication with others or—astonishing as it may seem that this would need to be stated—buy drugs on line. Away from the individual and onto organizations, the WHO has urged policymakers to invest in laboratory capacity and research to track increasing drug resistance as it happens, over time. Our leaders and governors were also advised to ensure that use of antibiotics is strictly regulated, something that can only be achieved through cooperation between themselves and the pharmaceutical industry. If innovation in research were encouraged, and new tools developed, the WHO argued, the threat might yet be contained.

5   But herein lies the biggest challenge of all. Antibiotic development has slowed down considerably over recent decades as the pharmaceutical industry becomes ever more governed by profit margins. Since they are used for a

relatively short time, and are often effective in curing the patient, antibiotics are nowhere near as lucrative as the drugs that treat long-term disorders, such as diabetes or asthma. Because medicines for chronic conditions are so much more profitable, this is where pharmaceutical companies invest their time and money. A further stumbling block is the relatively low cost of antibiotics, newer examples of which tend to cost a maximum of 1,000 to 3,000 per course. When compared with cancer chemotherapy, for example, a process of treatment that costs tens of thousands of pounds, the discrepancy becomes impossible to mend.

[6] As a race, humans have seen remarkable health benefits over the years as a huge number of illnesses have been treated by antibiotics, but we now face a global emergency as antibiotic resistant bacteria are beginning to emerge more rapidly and frequently than ever before. Not only has this created a potential health crisis, since we are increasingly unable to provide the sick with treatment as a result of worldwide overuse of these drugs, but it is also unlikely to be tackled any time soon, as the powerful pharmaceutical companies are primarily driven by profit and see little benefit in researching and creating new antibiotics. It simply does not work on the balance sheet, and so it falls to governments and individuals around the world to find ways to manage the crisis. Coordinating such efforts will not be easy.

Source: Fishman, Stephen. (2019, April). The growing global threat of antibiotics resistance. *Medical Advisor*, pp 49–50.

Task A | Reading Comprehension Strategy: Skipping over unknown words

Skipping unknown words is an effective reading skill when readers come to a new word. In some cases, it will be unnecessary to know the meaning of every word for understanding the key ideas in the context. Skipping reading, to some extent, helps readers get a general sense of the word from the passage.

Exercises

1. In this paragraph, every **fifth** word is missing. Read the paragraph and answer the questions. **DO NOT** try to guess the missing words.

   > Any substance that inhibits _____ growth and replication of _____ bacterium or kills it _____ can be called an _____. Antibiotics are a type _____ antimicrobial designed to target _____ infections within (or on) the _____. This makes antibiotics subtly _____ from the other main _____ of antibacterials widely used _____.
   >
   > Of course, bacteria are _____ the only microbes that _____ be harmful to us. _____ and viruses can also _____ a danger to humans, _____ they are targeted by _____ and antivirals, respectively. Only _____ that target bacteria are _____ antibiotics, while the name antimicrobial _____ an umbrella term for _____ that inhibits or kills _____ cells including antibiotics, antifungals, _____ and chemicals such as _____.
   >
   > Most antibiotics used today _____ produced in laboratories, but _____ are often based on _____ scientists have found in _____. Some microbes, for example, _____ substances specifically to kill _____ nearby bacteria in order _____ gain an advantage when _____ for food, water or _____ limited resources. However, some _____ only produce antibiotics in _____ laboratory.
   >
   > Find more on website: https://microbiologysociety.org/members-outreach-resources/outreach-resources/antibiotics-unearthed/antibiotics-and-antibiotic-resistance/what-are-antibiotics-and-how-do-they-work.html

   (1) What are antibiotics?

   (2) What are the functions of antibiotics?

   (3) Where are antibiotics produced?

2. Compare your answers with those of another student. Then discuss the following questions.

   (1) How many of the questions could you answer?

   (2) Did you need to know the missing words to understand the whole passage?

3. Now try to read the first paragraph in "The Growing Global Threat of Antibiotics Resistance". Remember to skip the unknown words and then summarize the main idea of the first paragraph.

Summary of Paragraph 1

Task B | Language Spotlight: Choosing the right level of formality

This text discussed ideas or problems that require specialist knowledge rather than general information, which requires the use of more formal language.

Match the formal words from Reading 2 to the following informal words in the left column.

1. advantage	
2. use	
3. happen	
4. process	
5. people	
6. greatly	

Task C | Vocabulary Practice: Words used to describe negative effects

1. Work with your partner and underline useful expressions that describe the negative effect of antibiotics resistance in Reading 1 and Reading 2.

Notes
Reading 1
Reading 2

2. Work with your partner and summarize the negative effect of antibiotics resistance. Remember to use the words above.

Notes

Task D | Critical Thinking: Inferences and evidence

> We make inferences all the time whether we realize it or not. Good readers make inferences while reading when we predict what will happen next or ask ourselves why a character is behaving a certain way.
>
> An inference is an educated guess that we make based on what we see or, while reading, the information provided in the text combined with our own experiences.
>
> Textual evidence is specific information from a text that we use to support our inferences.
>
> We use textual evidence to prove that our inferences are logical and accurate. In summary, when we try to fill in the gaps between what is explicitly said and what is implied, we are making inferences. We do this by making logical guesses based on what we observed and our own prior knowledge.

Discussion

Work with your partners and take the note of inferences on the impact of antibiotics resistance you are making. Then explain your reasoning by using textual evidence from the text.

Inference	Evidence	Inference	Evidence
e. g. I think ...	e. g. Because ...	e. g. I think ...	e. g. Because ...

Glossary of Unit 10

Reading 1

prolong
v. to lengthen in time; to cause to be or last longer
e. g. We prolonged our stay.

sinus
n. an abnormal passage leading from a suppurating cavity to the body surface
e. g. This normal variation in rhythm is known as sinus arrhythmia.

bloodstream
n. the blood flowing through the circulatory system
e. g. This drug works best if it is injected directly into the bloodstream.

septicemia
n. invasion of the bloodstream by virulent microorganisms from a focus of infection
e. g. The main emphasis of our research has shifted to the prevention of infection and septicemia.

prostate
n. a firm partly muscular chestnut sized gland in males at the neck of the urethra
e. g. The prostate is a small gland in men.

pneumonia
n. respiratory disease characterized by inflammation of the lung parenchyma (excluding the bronchi) with congestion caused by viruses or bacteria or irritants
e. g. Pneumonia carried him off last winter.

influenza
n. an acute febrile highly contagious viral disease
e. g. They should receive annual influenza vaccinations.

penicillin
n. any of various antibiotics obtained from penicillium molds (or produced synthetically) and used in the treatment of various infections and diseases
e. g. He gave me a second shot of penicillin.

boomerang
n. a curved piece of wood
e. g. The boomerang child phenomenon has become a social problem on a nationwide scale.

Reading 2

antibiotic
n. a chemical substance derivable from a mold or bacterium that can kill microorganisms and cure bacterial infections
e. g. When antibiotics were first discovered, they were called wonder drugs.

surgical
adj. of or relating to or involving or used in surgery
e. g. Acupuncture anesthesia is rapidly gaining ground in surgical operations.

curative

adj. tending to cure or restore to health

e. g. This is a hot spring credited with miraculous curative powers

prescribed

adj. conforming to set usage, procedure, or discipline

e. g. Books must be kept according to a prescribed form.

dosage

n. the quantity of an active agent (substance or radiation) taken in or absorbed at any one time

e. g. Do not exceed the recommended dosage.

replicate

v. to reproduce or make an exact copy of

e. g. Viruses usually replicate at the primary site of the entry.

infected

adj. containing or resulting from disease-causing organisms

e. g. The water was infected with germs.

contaminate

v. to make radioactive by adding radioactive material

e. g. All over the world, oil spills regularly contaminate coasts.

contained

adj. gotten under control

e. g. Contained with in the apparent peacefulness of the scene is a lurking threat.

pharmaceutical

adj. of or relating to pharmacy or pharmacists

e. g. She has donated money to establish a pharmaceutical laboratory.

Food and Disease

It is astonishing to contemplate how popular junk food has become, given that the first fast food restaurant in the US only opened its doors a mere century ago. Since then, high-calorie processed meals have taken over the world, with multinational restaurant chains aggressively chasing levels of growth that show no signs of slowing down. Much of this expansion is currently taking place in less developed parts of the world, where potential for customer loyalty is seen as easier to develop, but it is not just in these areas where such growth is visible. Indeed, a recent study from the University of Cambridge found that the number of takeaways in the United Kingdom rose by 45 per cent between 1997 and 2015. This explosion in the takeaway trade is not an inevitable outcome of what we call "progress". On the contrary, it comes in the face of an increasing body of evidence that we are heading for dietary disaster.

Yet, despite nutrition experts' best efforts to educate people about the dangers of a diet filled with processed food, it appears that the world doesn't want to listen. Medical specialists point out that, although eating too much unhealthy food is likely to be as dangerous in the long-term as smoking, regular consumption of high-calorie food has somehow become more socially acceptable than ever. While local authorities in some towns and cities have taken measures to combat the rise in this trend by limiting the number of fast food outlets permitted to be open simultaneously, critics argue that people have every right to make their own decisions about what they eat and how they choose to live. However, the way in which we have come to binge on takeaways isn't only a personal issue of weight gain, or of buying larger clothes. The consequences of mass overconsumption should strike fear into the hearts of everyone.

Research suggests that there is an evolutionary reason as to why people compulsively overeat—it is simply part of our innate behaviour. When humans evolved, we did not have the abundant supply of food that we enjoy today, and so eating was more about survival than pleasure. We became more likely to opt for high-calorie foods, with highfat content, that could sustain us through cold winters when the supply of nourishment became sparse. This explains why a 600-calorie burger seems so attractive: it awakens our primal side, makes us feel well fed, inspires contentment.

Processed food stimulates the reward response in our brains, so we feel compelled to overeat, and not necessarily in a healthy way. Junk food acts as a trigger for chemicals such as the "feel-good" dopamine to flood through the brain and induce a sensation of happiness.

Meanwhile, high amounts of sugar and sodium (one of the chemicals in salt and other ingredients of fast food) cause a huge surge in blood sugar, pushing it to unnatural levels. This occurs within the first few moments of eating a high-calorie meal. From there, routinely processing such high levels of sodium is impossible, and the body's organs are pushed beyond their natural working capacity in trying to do so. The kidneys can not remove all the excess salt from the blood, and thus an overdose of sodium causes the heart to pump faster while transporting blood through the veins. There are multiple dangers of highblood pressure, especially for the elderly and in the long-term. Sodium taken on in such quantities can lead to dehydration, a condition whose symptoms are extremely similar to hunger, and this leads to a painful truth: as soon you have finished your junk food meal, you immediately start to crave another. Thereafter, the body starts to digest the food. Usually, this takes between 4 and 12 hours, but with fast food, where the fat content is so much higher, the same process lasts at least three days.

A number of studies have shown how young people can become even more addicted to junk food than adults. When a child eats a burger, the same neurological processes occur as in their parents: their brain's reward system is awoken, dopamine is released, a spontaneous feeling of excitement results, their blood sugar rockets, and so on. An adult can apply their maturity to understand that this thrill is not entirely without drawbacks, and that they need to control their urge to eat more. However, a child can not necessarily see any negative consequences to this urge and the potential effects of their lack of self-control, so they find it far more difficult to exercise restraint and moderate their food consumption.

It is common to read or to hear criticism of the junk food industry that does so much to promote the over-consumption of its products. But it does not appear that any of this criticism is changing widespread dietary habits in any substantial way. What is more, the humble burger has been elevated to such a point that many people no longer see it as simple, on-the-go food. It has arguably become a stylish and aspirational part of one's daily diet. Consider, for example, how some television companies recently made several series of programme encouraging unnecessary overeating, in which the host devours dish after dish of unhealthy, fatty meals until they are full—and then far, far beyond. While such glamorization exists, it is difficult to see how our collective march towards a global obesity crisis can ever be halted.

Source: David, Thomas. (2018, June). Food and disease. *Health*, pp 98 – 99.